A Career Guide

for PhDs and PhD Candidates in English and Foreign Languages

Revised by

English Showalter

The Modern Language Association of America
New York 1985

Copyright © 1985 by The Modern Language Association of America

Library of Congress Cataloging-in-Publication Data

Showalter, English.
  A career guide for PhDs and PhD candidates in English and foreign languages.

  Includes bibliographies.
  1. Philology, Modern—Vocational guidance.
I. Modern Language Association of America. II. Title.
PB11.S54 1985   402.3'73   85-15527
ISBN 0-87352-146-3 (pbk.)

Published by The Modern Language Association of America
10 Astor Place, New York, New York 10003

CONTENTS

PREFACE

A wry observer of higher education once wondered what could be said in defense of an institution that had, at any given moment, half of its members searching for the other half. At the least one could argue that the search process must be important. And of course it is, since faculty and administrative appointments represent substantial, long-term financial commitments for a college or university and can influence its programs and reputation for many decades. The search process is also complex, shaped not only by an institution's desire to find the "best" people for faculty and administrative positions but also by its need to involve appropriate members of departments and related units and to observe affirmative action guidelines.

If you are a job seeker, the search is equally complex. To many new PhDs it may seem like a strange tribal rite with arcane customs and lore. In addition to the mystery of the process, those seeking faculty positions in English and foreign language departments must realize that since the early 1970s there have been more candidates than there are teaching positions, a situation likely to continue through the mid to late 1990s. Therefore, PhDs should also consider careers in other not-for-profit organizations, in business, or in government, where, since the early 1970s, increasing numbers of humanities PhDs have successfully established themselves.

You are the only person who can decide what you really want to do, and only when you make that decision can you find the job that suits you best. One key to success is planning ahead. You may not expect to finish taking graduate courses for several years, but whether you know it or not you are already a job candidate. What you do between now and the time you actually look at the lists of vacancies or begin writing to prospective employers is what you will put into your vita or résumé; what you do in your first job will be part of your qualifications for your second job; and so on. Being a student, getting a job, and doing the job are all part of the same activity: developing a career.

Graduate schools generally give students an excellent substantive education but often provide little instruction on professional matters. Even the most basic faculty responsibility, teaching, is often taught only by example. Many students are left to learn the ways of the profession for themselves. Values, attitudes, customs—a whole culture must be learned by osmosis, observation, and trial and error. Some PhD candidates absorb this professional ethos with little apparent effort; others do not. Even those who absorb it easily recall blunders they could have avoided if they had had more explicit direction. This guide cannot replace a mentor who knows both the candidate and the academic world, but it may supplement the advice of even the most conscientious advisers, who are likely to know little about employment outside the university, and it may demystify the workings of the profession for those who do not have mentors.

This revised version of the *Guide for Job Candidates and Department Chairmen in English and Foreign Languages*, which was first published in 1973, represents the thinking of several generations of members of the MLA Committee on Careers, of the Association of Departments of English (ADE), and of the Association of Departments of Foreign Languages (ADFL); the MLA's research about careers other than teaching; its experience with the Corporate Connections project; the advice of the Commission on the Status of Women, especially of Eve Kosofsky Sedgwick, who compiled twelve pages of useful suggestions, many of which have been incorporated verbatim; comments from many MLA members;

and information and insights gained by several members of the headquarters staff.

The purposes of this edition of the *Guide*, like those of earlier editions, are to make the job search more efficient and effective, to provide information for departmental advisers, and to encourage openness, courtesy, and good will throughout the process. The first chapter presents general considerations relevant to all graduate students, whether they choose to pursue a career in the academy, business, government, or associations and foundations. Since most PhDs intend to look first for jobs in the academy, the next and longest chapter takes up in detail the procedures for finding a teaching job in two- and four-year colleges and in universities; the third chapter provides additional information about two-year colleges; and the fourth covers the job search outside the academy. A concluding chapter makes recommendations for departments, both for hiring and for helping their students prepare for careers. Several appendixes give additional information, model documents, and the most recent statistical data on the job market for PhDs in English and foreign languages. Readers of this edition are invited to direct their comments about the *Guide* to the MLA Job Information Service.

1: GENERAL ADVICE FOR JOB SEEKERS

HOW TO BEGIN

You have already begun. As soon as you begin specializing in a course of study with the intention of making a career in that field, you also begin establishing a record of your abilities and accomplishments. The earlier you start planning how to use your time and efforts to best advantage, the easier you will find the last stages of looking for a job. If you have several years left in graduate school, you can do things right away to make your vita or résumé more impressive and thereby improve your chances of getting the job you want.

Consult the appropriate faculty members: the instructors in your classes, your thesis adviser(s), the graduate director, the placement officer, the department chair. Seek their advice on making yourself a better candidate; ask for their help on specific tasks like identifying an appropriate journal to which to submit an article. Try to get a fuller sense of the profession from them, and solicit their aid in learning about careers outside the academic world. One way to do this is to ask them about their own careers. Consultation not only gets you expert advice but also makes you known to members of the faculty and interests them in your situation and progress. Remember, however, that they are busy people; do not make excessive demands on their time or waste it with pointless meetings.

Read about the profession and about job hunting. This *Guide* is a good place to start, but read some of the works listed in chapter 4 as well. Be sure to learn something about professions other than college teaching. You cannot choose a career intelligently without some knowledge of the range of opportunities open to you. Moreover, many of the principles that apply to job hunting in business also succeed in the academic world. Talk with your friends enrolled in other graduate programs and with as many other people as you can about their work in business, government, not-for-profit organizations, and other kinds of employment.

Gain some teaching experience as early as possible. If your department has no systematic provision for supervision and evaluation, invite the appropriate faculty members to visit your classes and advise you on your teaching. Their evaluations will help make you a better teacher, and they will be able to write more persuasive letters of recommendation for you.

Develop more than one area of expertise. Academics can be pigeonholed for life by their choice of a thesis topic. Even when you are a candidate for a teaching position in your specialty, the ability to do something more will help distinguish you from other candidates. Become knowledgeable about a field currently in demand, such as writing, women's studies, computer-aided instruction, or foreign language for business uses.

In your classes, treat your term papers as possible articles. Conceive of them as the original work of a professional addressing an audience of peers. Write them in the style and format of journal articles. If they seem to have promise, revise them according to the criticism of the professor and send them to an appropriate journal. You may not have your first effort accepted for publication, but you will be learning the style and the procedures. You may well receive valuable critiques from the journal editors. If you think your idea is a good one, do not be discouraged by an initial rejection; revise again, and submit the essay again somewhere else. If all goes well, you will have some publications to list on your vita before you have completed your degree; at the least, you will have a sample

1

of your work to show to prospective employers, you can list such papers on your vita as "submitted for publication," and you will have gained valuable experience.

Some classwork not suitable for publication may still form the basis for a conference paper. A typical conference paper takes twenty minutes to read; for most people, that means a maximum of ten double-spaced pages. As with an article, if your paper is accepted, you have a significant accomplishment to add to your vita; at worst, you will have acquired experience. In both cases, you bring yourself to the attention of colleagues outside your own campus, to some extent even if your work is turned down. It is through such exposure that you build a network of professional colleagues and find new mentors.

You should take advantage of the opportunity to attend lectures by visiting professors in your field, defined in the broadest sense. Not only will this enhance your understanding of the subject, it will also allow you to meet more people in the field. Inform yourself about the speaker and the topic ahead of time, and think of questions to ask. The best questions are not those that challenge or criticize but rather those that invite the lecturer to expand and elaborate. Look for a chance to meet and talk to the speaker afterward. If the person is in an area close to yours, you may mention the work you are doing. Do not press yourself on visitors too hard; you need only make a contact and establish the basis for some future exchange.

If there is a graduate students' association in your department, participate actively in it. If students give reports on their work in progress, volunteer to give one. Propose someone to be invited as a guest speaker, and take charge of organizing the event, arranging for the room, introducing the guest, hosting a reception afterwards. Some of the best speakers are young scholars who have just published their first book. They will be flattered by the invitation, grateful for the opportunity to build their reputation, more likely to be available, and often more disposed to work on producing a really good talk.

Whenever a scholarly conference in your field takes place on your campus or nearby, attend. These conferences range from one-time-only events commemorating anniversaries to regular meetings on fairly narrow themes to annual meetings of associations like the MLA and the regional MLAs. To get a feel for them, you may prefer to begin with a smaller one close to your campus; registration will probably cost less, and you will have lower transportation and lodging costs. Usually, graduate students benefit from lower rates. Sometimes, by working on the arrangements, you may be able to gain valuable experience and also to attend free. Once you have seen what conferences are like, you should try to give a paper somewhere. By the time you consider attending the MLA's annual convention for job interviews, you ought to feel at home in a scholarly meeting.

Many graduate departments sponsor a journal or serve as the headquarters for a scholarly society. Inquire about working for them. You will learn something about editing and management and will have opportunities for meeting people at other institutions.

All these suggestions can be acted on quickly and should grow naturally out of your course work and research interests. You will want to know what others are working on and thinking about. You may feel uncomfortable at first approaching scholars who are not your professors, but common intellectual interests provide a basis for such discussions, and scholarly activities are designed to provide opportunities for them.

Since all these activities are associated with graduate work, their most obvious relevance is to an academic career. Each one, however, affords some experience that will have value in nonteaching jobs as well. In the section on résumés, you will see how to classify the various activities under headings like "Writing," "Editing," "Managerial," "Communications," "Analytical," and "Personnel." The efforts you make to broaden your range of abilities will supply evidence of initiative. In addition, meeting with people in business, government, and other fields can help you decide how to orient your career and at the same time help allay employers' fears that you have decided to look at jobs outside the academy only as a desperate last resort.

- Start now.
- Consult.
- Read about the teaching profession, about other professions, and about job hunting.
- Get teaching experience early.
- Submit an article for publication.
- Begin going to conferences and giving papers.
- Look for professional opportunities in your department.
- Develop more than one specialty.

PREPARING FOR THE FIRST JOB SEARCH
When

At some point in your career it will be time to leave graduate school and find a job. In the past this moment normally arrived soon after the comprehensive examination; the student by then had completed all residency and credit requirements, and passage of the exam signified readiness to write the dissertation. More recently, most PhD candidates have remained at the graduate institutions, often as part-time teachers, while they worked on their dissertations. You should try to stay on campus until work on the thesis is well under way; afterward, as an ABD (that is, someone who has completed all requirements but the dissertation), you can presumably work independently most of the time and send chapters to your director at intervals for criticism and advice. The nature of the thesis may affect your freedom; someone doing extensive research or using primary sources would require access to a major library and might not be able to work effectively in a small college in a remote area.

You will need to plan ahead for the year when you actually expect to look for openings and submit applications. The academic hiring cycle coincides roughly with the academic year, beginning in September and ending in May or June. Some important steps should be taken in the spring preceding that year, however, so it is to your advantage to make a firm decision around January that you will begin looking systematically in the fall and to set up certain parts of your campaign right away.

Outside higher education, job hunting is less seasonal and less organized across the entire field. Hiring takes place whenever a vacancy occurs or a new position develops, and searching for a job candidate usually takes far less time than the academic year faculties devote to it. Although advance preparation is equally important in all areas of employment, the highly defined structure of the academic job market makes it easier to describe systematically. Most of the stages have an equivalent in other fields, though, as chapter 4 explains.

Vita

Whatever sort of job you look for, you will need a document containing a record of what you have done and a description of what you can do. In the academic world, this document is called a curriculum vitae, vita, or cv; in other fields of employment it is called a résumé. The formats vary according to the kind of job you are applying for (the specific variations will be explained in the following chapters); in all cases, however, it is crucial to follow the customary format and to prepare the document neatly, with professional-quality typing and copying. Even before this document is read, its appearance will make an impression. Take some care in preparing it, and do not economize on typing and copying.

Obviously, neatness and perfect typing will not compensate for a lack of substance. The previous section contained suggestions for generating content to put in a vita or résumé. If you have weak credentials, perhaps you ought to delay the job search another year. Placement counselors, however, can often bring to light items that candidates overlook; get some advice before you make your decision. If you assess your status in January, moreover, you will have time to produce some material before September, when you actually need to have the document ready.

Under no circumstances should you pad the vita or résumé with trivial or irrelevant items. Length is no asset if the reader finds the content unimpressive. You must consider the perspective of the person who will read the document: a personnel officer in a business firm would want to know you have writing skills and professional publications but will have no interest in a list of scholarly articles, whereas a college department chair would find it evasive if the articles were not listed. Your work advising a student newspaper might be important to a community college department, but probably not to a university.

References

You will also need to have some letters of recommendation, or at least the names of people willing to write letters if asked. It is difficult to offer general suggestions about whom to approach; to some extent, that decision must depend on the type of job you want, maybe even the specific job. A letter carries much more weight if the author is personally known to the people who read it. Students tend to want letters from the most famous members of the faculty; if Professor Superstar writes on behalf of fifteen or twenty students every year, though, a less prominent colleague who writes for only two or three may serve you better. Someone who knows you well is certainly preferable to someone, however celebrated and powerful, who can write about you only in vague generalities.

One thing is absolutely certain: you cannot wait until the last minute to line up your references. If you do nothing else in your years of graduate study, you must earn the support of at least four people with established reputations. If you have not done that, either you have begun job hunting too soon or else you have chosen the wrong career. Consult with your thesis adviser and the department chair about the choice of references. Courtesy requires that you ask the permission of those you list as references before you list them, and you should be sensitive to any sign of reluctance. Very few people will write negative letters, if they agree willingly to write; at worst they will fill their letter with vague clichés. Someone who begs off, claiming to be too busy or not to know you well enough, should not be pressed, no matter how flimsy the excuse seems to you.

Under federal law, certain letters of recommendation cannot be kept confidential from their subject unless the subject has signed a waiver. University placement offices often have a form for letters of recommendation, with the waiver printed on it. Some experienced people in the field urge candidates to sign the waiver and give up their right to see the letter. They argue that students who insist on the right to see their letters of recommendation may appear insecure and suspicious and may annoy their own supporters. Many people will simply refuse to write without the waiver, and those who write may resort to bland, cautious comments of little use. Others, however, think that it is never inappropriate to avail yourself of your legal rights. You should know that if employers feel a need to circumvent this law, they have the right to telephone and may do so. There is certainly no reason for you to raise the issue of the waiver, but you should think about it and make up your mind about what to do, in case it comes up.

Cover Letter

Whenever you send the vita or résumé to a prospective employer, you must accompany it with a letter. In the academic world, this letter is usually called a letter of application; in business it is called a cover letter. Here again, appearance is extremely important; the letter should be neatly typed on good stationery, a letterhead if appropriate. Although the vita or résumé may be photocopied, these letters should be written individually for each job you apply for. The letter offers you your only chance to explain why your skills and interests make you a strong candidate for this particular job. Do not waste that chance by sending a form letter.

Departmental Services

Many departments offer services for students who are looking for jobs. Some possibilities include a late spring meeting at which prospective job hunters, veterans of the previous year's efforts, and younger faculty members talk together; an early fall meeting at which the department chair, graduate director, or placement officer goes over specifics; an individual conference with the faculty member heading the department's placement effort; and a meeting before the MLA convention to practice with mock interviews.

Make use of whatever opportunities exist. The final section of this *Guide* lists suggestions for how departments can assist their students; if your department has not instituted some services that you think might be helpful, get together with other job candidates and ask that it do so.

Above all, keep your advisers informed. Let them know as soon as you decide to look; ask them for help with any problems and advice on any questions; tell them about any response you get from a prospective employer; discuss any plans you have. If nothing seems to be happening, go over your situation with them. Throughout your career, success will depend on the support of colleagues and mentors.

- Allow plenty of time for the actual job search.
- Prepare your vita or résumé in advance.
- Pay attention to appearance.
- Pay attention to the audience.
- Line up your letters of recommendation.
- Write letters of application or cover letters individually.
- Make use of departmental services.
- Keep your advisers informed.

LETTERS OF APPLICATION

You may hear of job openings in various ways. For academic jobs in language and literature departments, the MLA *Job Information Lists* give the most convenient and reliable information (see pp. 13-14 for complete information). As soon as possible after the *Lists* appear, you should send letters of application in response to all the appropriate announcements. For other kinds of jobs, you may have to pursue leads from a variety of sources, including the placement office, classified ads, personal contacts, and visits to potential employers. Sooner or later, however, you will probably write a letter of application to some of them.

In all situations, letters should be individually written and typed neatly in correct business format. Although each letter ought to be specifically related to the particular job, much of the information will be the same in all of them. Do not use a photocopied letter with spaces filled in. A word processor, of course, will make writing these letters much easier. If you are entitled to use a letterhead from your department, do so.

The letter is intended to present you and your qualifications crisply and attractively. It should address itself explicitly to the requirements stated in the announcement. In general, it should be precise, well structured, and appropriately styled. Remember that its appearance, manner of expression, and tone will constitute the first personal impression you make.

In the heading of the letter, give the address at which you wish to receive mail; this address should also be on your vita. On the left, above the salutation, place the name and address of the person to whom you are writing. Whenever possible, address the letter to an individual, not simply to the office.

In the first paragraph, state what job announcement you are responding to; mention both the title of the job and the place where you saw the ad, or explain how you heard of it. In the second paragraph, present yourself, mentioning your degree status and institution or your current job (if it is relevant—do not say that you are working in a fast-food restaurant, for example, or that you are unemployed). Assert your eligibility for the job, and mention the aspects of your background that meet the specific requirements in the job announcement.

Avoid simply repeating the information on your vita. Highlight the strong points and elaborate on them. If, for example, the job calls for specialty in a century and your thesis falls within the period, describe what you are writing about. If the job calls for expertise in teaching a certain area, give some details about the courses you have taught. You should not apply for positions for which you are clearly not qualified, but the number of teaching jobs is too small to ignore those for which your qualifications are close but not perfect. For nonacademic jobs, discuss the value of your graduate education for the field you hope to enter. You should expect some skepticism about the suitability of graduate school as a preparation for other careers. Never lie or falsify your preparation, but put the best face on what you have done and avoid self-deprecation. A positive attitude will be especially important in presenting graduate work to nonacademic employers. Before you write the letter, visit the library and consult your faculty advisers and friends to learn whatever you can about the employer. Anything you can cite that makes this job special to you would improve your chances.

In the closing paragraphs, take care of the practical matters. Mention the vita and any other enclosures. Explain where your dossier is on file, and how it can be obtained; if you have to order it yourself, offer to do so. For academic positions, indicate your willingness to be interviewed at the MLA convention, and mention any other conventions or meetings you plan to attend. If you know your address and phone number for forthcoming holidays, it is a good idea to give them. Have a chapter of your dissertation and/or some other substantial piece of writing ready to send; describe what you have, and offer to send it on request.

Enclose a stamped, self-addressed postcard with which your application can be acknowledged. Be sure to put some identification on the card so that you will know who has returned it, in the event it is simply dropped in the mail. Mention the card in your letter, and ask whether it could be used to tell you when you might have further word.

Keep copies of your letters. It will be useful to review what you have already said before you go to an interview, and it is important to have some record of what jobs you have applied for. You may need to write more letters later, and the copies can serve as models. Finally, sometimes letters get lost in the mail, and you may have to redo the same letter.

Show your letters of application to your adviser before you send them, and incorporate any recommended changes. See the samples in appendix C.

- Send letters of application promptly.
- Write each letter individually.
- Pay attention to the appearance of the letters.
- Highlight your qualifications for the particular job.
- Avoid simply repeating your vita; amplify, explain, give new information.
- Tailor your letter to the job.
- Do not apply for jobs for which you lack the qualifications.
- Enclose a stamped, self-addressed card for acknowledgment.
- Keep a copy of each letter.
- Have your adviser check your letters of application before you send them.

What Happens Next

Candidates for jobs in colleges and universities tend to hear of many openings all at once, to apply for several at a time, and then to hear the results, good or bad, within a brief span. Outside academe, cycles are more varied, if, indeed, hiring follows a cycle at all.

Within a couple of weeks, you should receive the acknowledgment card; if it does not come back, telephone to make sure your letter arrived. Some departments will give you specific dates for the further stages of the hiring procedure; others will simply return the card. Some may even notify you by return mail that you do not qualify as a candidate, giving little or no additional explanation.

Do not become discouraged or depressed by early negative responses; remember that the rejections always come first. The competition is intense and all but one of the applicants for any given job must be turned down at some point. It is in fact a courtesy to the unsuccessful applicants to notify them as soon as possible. Departments usually make an effort to communicate this disappointing news as tactfully as possible, but most will give only vague and general reasons, frequently in a form letter. Often the letter will say something like "Your qualifications do not fit our needs," which may seem quite untrue to you, but do not waste your time writing back. Occasionally you may get an insensitively worded rejection; resist the impulse to dash off a rejoinder, try not to let it bother you, and console yourself with the thought that you would not have wanted to work with such people anyway.

The earliest favorable responses will probably be requests for your dossier. If you have to order it from the placement office or authorize its release, do so as promptly as possible. When you have done so, send the requesting department a note to inform them. Repeat in this note the addresses and telephone numbers where you can be reached in the weeks ahead, especially leading up to the MLA convention. Notify your own department and your adviser about any dossier requests; your professors may be able to give you useful advice about the job and may be willing to send a supporting note or make a telephone call to a colleague on that campus. Meanwhile you should begin to prepare yourself by doing some additional research on the institution; see the section on preparing for interviews (pp. 23–24).

Requests for the dossier indicate some interest, but only at the most tentative level. You may hear nothing more for a long time, and you may then be notified that you are no longer a candidate. If you were given a timetable and you do not hear when you should, feel free to call and ask what your status is and when you can expect to hear something more. You may not improve your situation, but you can probably clarify it. In the fall, preceding the MLA convention, call at least several days before the end of classes. At other times, if no date has been set, you should feel free to telephone after a month of silence following the acknowledgment of your initial application. In the business world, follow-up telephone calls should be made earlier and more persistently.

If your dossier confirms your qualifications for the job, you may then be invited to an interview. This invitation expresses real interest on the part of an academic department. Conducting interviews is expensive, time-consuming, and demanding when done with care; only those with a real chance at the job are likely to be invited. The interview is also one of the most important elements in the screening process. You should respond favorably to any invitations and—if the interview is to take place at the MLA convention or if the institution is not far from your own—should be willing to bear some inconvenience and expense to accommodate the search committee or the head of the hiring department. As soon as you have scheduled an interview, you should learn more about the school and the members of the department. Outside the academic world almost all interviewing is done at the site of the job (although businesses and government agencies may send recruiters to campuses) and usually at the candidate's expense, at least for entry-level positions. The significance of being interviewed may also vary widely from one situation to another. It is, however, always a necessary step and usually a positive sign.

Inevitably, much of your time will be spent waiting. The stress of living in uncertainty, of building up hopes and having them dashed, can wreck your morale. The best way to ward off depression is to use the time making yourself a better candidate. Don't just wait; involve yourself in some of the activities described in the first part of this chapter. Don't try to keep your anxiety to yourself; talk to your advisers, your colleagues, and your friends. Don't stake all your hopes on one kind of job; make some contingency plans. The search for the first job is in many ways the hardest, but you will find the pattern repeated many times in an academic career, as you look for other jobs, watch the mail for news of your manuscript, scan the journals for reviews of your book, wait for the announcements of the fellowship winners, and await decisions on promotion and tenure. The search and the waiting are part of the career.

- Do not be discouraged by early negative responses.
- Keep your morale up.

- React promptly to positive responses.
- Do not just wait; use the time constructively.

Conventions

The conventions of professional associations and learned societies play an important role in the careers of most academics. Graduate students often attend primarily to participate in the job service, especially to be available for interviews. Many other useful activities take place at conventions, however, and you should not limit your attention to job hunting. In fact, the MLA convention is well worth attending, whether or not you have interviews scheduled and whether or not you expect to look for a teaching job in the future. Conventions offer unique opportunities for professional networking, that is, for establishing and consolidating with colleagues from other campuses the same sort of personal contacts you have with your teachers, your fellow students, and eventually your departmental colleagues. Actually, job hunting is only a particularly intense and formal kind of networking.

The first part of this chapter offers some suggestions for learning about conventions and other scholarly meetings without great expense; it is a good idea to become familiar with conventions before you attend as a job seeker. This section will concentrate on the MLA's annual convention, which is the principal interview site for chairs and candidates in language and literature departments. The MLA convention is one of the largest in the academic world, with an average attendance of seven to ten thousand people. It meets every year on the same dates, 27 to 30 December, but in different cities. You need not be an MLA member to attend, although members enjoy advantageous registration rates and are sure to receive the announcements in good time. Information on membership is printed regularly in *PMLA*; it can also be obtained by writing to MLA headquarters. Dues for students are reasonable, and you will find many advantages in joining the MLA long before you complete your dissertation. The MLA offers favorable hotel rates for those who preregister and frequently negotiates special transportation rates as well. Members receive up-to-date information on all aspects of the convention as a matter of course in the early fall.

A typical MLA convention program, which appears as the November issue of *PMLA*, lists almost seven hundred functions, most of which are literary or pedagogical sessions where scholars and teachers give papers. In addition, a number of sessions every year are devoted to advising job candidates, and many others deal with practical professional matters. The program also includes a large number of social functions that, although they may place limits on attendance, are all open to all registrants on a first-come, first-served basis.

As a newcomer to the profession, you would be well advised to pay special attention to the sessions on the profession itself. The MLA-sponsored Association of Departments of English (ADE) and Association of Departments of Foreign Languages (ADFL) conduct workshops at the start of the convention to counsel job candidates. Some other typical subjects for professional sessions would include part-time teachers, independent scholars, translation as a profession, book reviewing, leaving the academy, hiring criteria, women in the profession, faculty in two-year colleges, business careers for PhDs, peer evaluation, libraries, scholarly publishing, grants, fellowships, and publishing your first book. In all these sessions, you can get advice directly from experts on the practical questions you have to face as an academic or as a PhD in a nonacademic job.

9

The traditional sessions are organized around a subject. The different structures behind the sessions are explained in the Directory issue of *PMLA* ("Procedures for Organizing Meetings at the MLA Convention and Policies for MLA Divisions and Discussion Groups") and are indicated in the program. If you plan only to attend, you may not be able to distinguish among them most of the time. The typical session has a presiding officer and three speakers; their names and the titles of their papers are given in the program. If you want to hear one of the papers, you simply wear your badge proving that you have registered, walk in, and sit down. Many people in the audience come and go between speakers.

If there is discussion afterward, it is a good idea to ask a question, but MLA convention sessions usually do not evoke the sort of give-and-take from the audience that arises in more cohesive groups on a campus, for example, or at a small colloquium on a single subject. It is frequently more productive to go up to the rostrum afterward, introduce yourself to the speakers and organizers, ask questions then, mention your own interests in the area, and—especially in sessions sponsored by a division—inquire about the next year's program. Many sessions welcome submissions from anyone. The names and addresses of organizers and the topics are published in the *MLA Newsletter*, with the largest number appearing in the Spring issue. Early planning is essential, as choices have to be made by early April for the convention the following December. Often the subject for the following year is announced during a session, so you may get some useful guidance and a head start by being there.

A large group of meetings are called special sessions. Each has been organized by a member who chose the topic, found the speakers, and submitted a proposal to the Program Committee. Any member may propose a special session on any subject; the guidelines are printed in the Directory issue of *PMLA*. Even though the MLA convention is large, complex, and intimidating, it offers a remarkable range of opportunities for anyone to gain a place on the program. By participating in the program, you identify yourself to colleagues as being interested in your field, and you will have something like an interview with everyone in the audience. At your first convention, you will probably want mainly to observe. As soon as possible, however, you should begin investigating the possibility of presenting a paper yourself.

The new books, audiovisual equipment, computers, and other displays attract most members to the exhibit area at least once during the convention. Books are usually on sale at substantial discounts, and some are given away. Many presses have prepublication copies. Visiting the exhibits is, in short, an easy way to keep up to date with trends in your field, in scholarly books, in textbooks, and in teaching aids. Do not overlook the opportunity to meet some of the university-press editors, who usually attend and are often waiting in their booths to talk to anyone who walks by. If you plan to try to publish your thesis, you can discuss your project with some of the key people who will decide whether to accept it. If you can get their advice ahead of time, it will greatly improve your chances of success.

The social events fall into three categories: cash bars, prepaid events where reservations are required, and private parties. Publishers and large departments often throw parties in their suites; your chances of being invited depend on knowing or meeting the right person. Some reserved events are announced in the program, which will give information on how to reserve a place; others are arranged by allied organizations meeting with the MLA, and you will probably have to be a member of that organization to receive the necessary information. If you are working in a field that sponsors such an event, you will find the annual lunch or dinner the fastest possible way to get to know most of the scholars in the field. The cash bars are open to everyone; the drinks are expensive, but admission is free and you do not have to buy a drink. Departments often sponsor cash bars for the faculty, students, alumnae, alumni, and friends; anyone can qualify as a friend. If a group with an interest close to yours sponsors a cash bar, you have an easy way to meet many of your professional colleagues quickly. Make a point of introducing yourself to some new people; everyone has a name tag, which makes it simple. If you do not see any familiar names or faces, find someone else who is standing alone and start a conversation. In such a self-selecting group, anyone you meet you are likely to meet again.

- Attend an MLA convention before you go as a job seeker.
- Take advantage of the sessions on professional topics.
- Consider giving a paper.
- Look for ways to meet colleagues in your field.

2: THE ACADEMIC JOB SEARCH

HOW LONG DOES THE JOB SEARCH TAKE?

The development of a career begins from the moment you decide on a field of interest. All your time in graduate school, both in class and out, can be devoted to professional preparation and training. When the time comes to leave graduate school and look actively for a job, you should start assembling your credentials and consulting your advisers early in the spring preceding the academic year in which you hope to apply for jobs.

Not long ago, candidates typically completed the active part of the job search within one year. After some preparation in the spring, they sent out applications in the fall, were interviewed at the MLA convention in December, perhaps visited the campus in January or February, and received an offer soon afterward. Such a sequence rarely occurs these days.

Because of the financial difficulties that most institutions face, the final authorization for hiring frequently comes much later in the year than it used to. As a result, many job offers are made late in the spring and over the summer. Moreover, appointments to part-time and temporary positions are commonly made after students have registered for the courses, that is, in August or September; only then do administrators know for sure that enrollments justify additional hiring.

With jobs scarce and competition for them intense, many candidates find no teaching job at all in their first year of looking. Since many jobs are temporary, some of the same candidates return to the job market year after year. In the academic world, the job hunt does not really end until one has received tenure; even then, continued advancement may depend on receiving offers from other institutions. In a real sense, the job hunt and the job are the same thing.

You should therefore be prepared to spend several years, if necessary. You should not become discouraged if your first efforts meet with little success, and you should not relax into complacency when you find your first job. Especially at the beginning, you should try to arrange a fallback plan: for example, find out whether your home institution will allow you another year as a teaching assistant or coadjutant, look into fellowships, investigate the opportunities for other kinds of employment. None of this time need be considered wasted or lost; use it to gain experience and to build up your vita.

The poor job market has stretched the period of apprenticeship for academics to a barely tolerable length. Language and literature students spend an average of about ten years in graduate school before receiving the doctorate. Many then spend several more years employed in non-tenure-track jobs. When they finally receive a tenure-track appointment, they usually must spend six years before coming up for promotion; often, if they are released without tenure from the first such job, they waive the seniority so as not to come up for review too soon at the next one. Not many people survive this sort of endurance test, but there are more and more assistant professors in their forties, still awaiting a final tenure decision.

Some PhD candidates think it is advantageous not to earn their degree too quickly, so as to prolong their eligibility for student subsidies and to have more time to build up a dossier. This is a dubious strategy, and candidates who consider waiving prior service or who find themselves moving from one non-tenure-track job to another should entertain the same doubts. If you feel confident that you are improving your qualifications each year and not just putting in time, then you have good reason to delay entering the job market or to continue in a non-tenure-track status. If you are not improving your credentials in any demonstrable way, however, then you should give serious thought to looking for jobs in other fields. Discuss your situation with a professional job counselor. The longer you delay the move, the more painful it will probably seem and the less time you will have to move ahead in a more rewarding career.

However long it takes to get the job, you should regard the time as a period of investment in your future. Many colleges, universities, foundations, and government agencies provide financial assistance for certain professional activities, such as travel to conventions, research, and publication costs. Obviously, you should use these resources as much as possible, but when no assistance is available, you should be ready to pay such expenses yourself. Many other important professional activities (such as having your vita typed) are not usually eligible for support, and many expenses (such as suitable clothes) are only indirectly connected to professional needs. Meeting such expenses will certainly require sacrifices from candidates living on the scandalously low salaries of part-time and junior faculty in humanities departments. It is, however, a self-defeating false economy to refuse to invest in the things you need to get a job and have a successful career.

- Job hunting and doing the job are often the same activity.
- Be prepared to stay on the job market for several years.
- Do not be discouraged too early; offers often come late in the summer.
- Use the time of your search, apprenticeship, and probation to improve your credentials.
- Review your situation every year; do not persist in a choice that is not working out for you.

Job Information Lists

In the early fall, you will begin applying for jobs. As the first chapter explains, you initiate the process by writing a letter and sending a vita to a department looking for a person with your qualifications. How do you know what departments have openings and what sort of person they are looking for? There are several possible sources. The *Chronicle of Higher Education* carries faculty job announcements in each weekly issue; the *New York Times* also carries some in the Sunday "Week in Review" section, and the openings are not limited to the New York area. Sometimes a hiring department will write directly to graduate departments; an announcement may be posted, or a member of the faculty may tell you about a vacancy. By far the most important source of job information for candidates in language, literature, and some related fields is the *MLA Job Information Lists*.

The MLA publishes two *Lists*, one for English and one for foreign languages. Their aim is to provide candidates with employment information that is as complete and up-to-date as possible. The *Lists* appear four times a year—in October, December, February, and April—and are sent by first-class mail to subscribers in the United States and Canada and by airmail to subscribers overseas. There is also a summer supplement. The *Lists* are sent to all departments that join either the ADE or the ADFL. Students in graduate departments or job seekers employed by a department may therefore be able to consult the *Lists* in the department office. Individual subscriptions are also available; write to the MLA for information on rates. Anyone looking for a faculty position in English or foreign languages or in related fields like comparative literature, ethnic studies, women's studies, linguistics, or classics should obtain access to the *Job Information Lists* as early as possible in the search and read each issue carefully as soon as it appears.

The main body of each *List* consists of a series of statements from department chairs on definite or possible openings or any other information (change in deadline date, new job description, etc.) that might be of interest to a job seeker. The October and February issues also list departments reporting no vacancy. Two-year colleges may advertise openings in any *List*, and information is especially solicited from them for the February issue. Canadian departments are regularly included. There are also usually numerous listings for overseas appointments and jobs in business, government, or other fields, although the MLA cannot solicit from those sectors as systematically as from college departments.

While it may seem tedious and even discouraging to read through the entire *List* when only a few definite vacancies are advertised in an individual candidate's field, the *Lists* aim to spare the job seeker the expense and trouble of making useless applications. When you know that a department is looking for someone with your qualifications, you can present yourself more effectively in a letter of application and prepare yourself better for interviews.

The *Lists* are also intended to promote open employment practices. By making this service available free of charge to hiring departments, the MLA encourages the listing of all vacancies of the open market. You should be aware, however, that the MLA cannot compel departments to submit listings and does not publish any announcements except those submitted by employers. For various reasons, some departments do not use the *Lists* and prefer to hire through some other channel, such as the "old boys' network." On the whole, however, the *Lists* are a reliable guide to employment opportunities in colleges and universities.

In compiling the *Lists*, the MLA encourages departments to follow the generally accepted procedures of the profession to ensure fair and courteous treatment of all candidates. The *Lists* will not carry notices containing illegal conditions or offensive language. The MLA cannot supervise the departments' conduct in carrying out the search, however, or investigate complaints and grievances. Abuses are in fact rare. Overwhelmingly, departments have cooperated with efforts to make the treatment of candidates fairer and their experience less stressful.

- Get access to the *MLA Job Information Lists* and other sources of job announcements.
- Keep up to date with the latest announcements.

WHERE TO APPLY

In general, write only to institutions that seem to be looking for a person with your qualifications. Of course, if your adviser or department chair has learned of a vacancy and urges you to apply to a specific department, you should do so, even if the department has announced no vacancy. The opening may have occurred after the last deadline, or you may be fortunate enough to benefit from a network.

You should be liberal, although not dishonest, in matching your qualifications to a job description. If you have some experience in a field, even though you do not regard it as your specialty, you should apply for jobs in it—provided, of course, that you are willing to teach in that field if you get the job. Especially when the advertisement seems impre-

14

cise, the department may be more interested in a good person than in a particular specialty. If you are in doubt, consult your adviser, but in general you should apply for any job that you think your experience qualifies you for.

Do not waste your time writing blindly to departments that have announced no vacancy. The only exception to this principle is that if for some reason you will be geographically bound to a certain area—because your spouse has a job there, for example—then you may write to the departments in the area, explaining the situation and announcing your availability for last-minute and part-time openings.

In view of the difficult job market, you should be prepared to write to a range of institutions in different locations. Obviously, family circumstances might limit your freedom, but you must bear in mind that many of your rivals for jobs may have no such limits or may be willing to accept a "commuter marriage." Similarly, you may feel obligated to rule out certain institutions, such as church-affiliated colleges with well-defined curricular restrictions or codes of behavior that you do not honestly believe you can accept. You ought to recognize from the start that such limitations give you a handicap in an already difficult situation. Neither prospective employers nor your own mentors are likely to have much patience with you if you disdain jobs simply because you prefer a certain type of school or a certain region—especially if, as is usually the case, the type of school and the region you prefer are those that most candidates consider desirable.

Academic jobs are unusual in their specificity of field, of place, and of hiring time. In most professions, skills are thought to be more adaptable, there are more possible employment opportunities in any given area, and hiring goes on all the time as former employees leave or business expands. Indeed, the skills you have as a PhD will probably seem useful for a greater range of jobs in business or government than in education; that is one reason why you ought to keep those options in mind. See chapter 4 for specific advice on applying for such jobs.

Conversely, if you are looking for jobs in colleges and universities, you must find ways to deal with the conditions of the job market; you may have little choice about the region or the type of institution where you take your first job. You can become qualified in more than one field, so as to maximize your opportunities, but to get started you must be prepared to go where the job is. If you continue to improve your qualifications, you will probably have chances to move later on, to institutions that are, from your point of view, more prestigious, better located, or at least more generous.

- Apply only for advertised vacancies.
- Be as flexible as possible about region, type of institution, etc.
- If some unavoidable circumstance restricts your freedom to apply for all jobs in your field, assess your career prospects carefully, recognizing that you suffer from a certain handicap.

COVER LETTER

Follow the general advice in chapter 1 on writing a cover letter or letter of application. Write each one separately, and be sure it is neat and well typed in the proper format.

In the salutation, if the job announcement gives a name but no title for the chair or head of the search committee, use "Professor," which is appropriate for all ranks. If no name is given, either omit the salutation entirely or use "To the head of the search committee," or whatever other title is given in the announcement. A salutation like "Dear Sir," implying that the addressee is male, will sound wrong to about half the people likely to see your letter; some people, however, dislike recent coinages such as "chairperson." If you are writing at your adviser's informal suggestion or on your own initiative, not in response to an advertisement, look up the department chair's name in the MLA Directory or the college catalog.

Besides highlighting the strengths of your vita, you will probably want to mention some qualifications that your vita does not show clearly. For example, your thesis title may suggest specialization in one century, whereas the approach you use may make you equally qualified to teach the century preceding or following, or a course title may give no indication that one component dealt with the area the job calls for.

Never lie or falsify your credentials, but put the best face on what you have done. Avoid self-disparagement: do not say, "I am not really a specialist in the Enlightenment, but . . ." or "Although I have never taught the eighteenth century, . . ."; instead say, "I took a course on the Enlightenment with Professor Famous and wrote essays on Hume and Rousseau" or "As part of the introduction-to-literature course, I taught Swift, Pope, and Fielding."

You may be able to call attention to some experience or interest that is not suitable for inclusion on a vita but that seems relevant to the particular job. For an opening in a predominantly engineering school, for example, any technical or scientific training you have had might equip you better to teach those students. For an opening in a school with a religious affiliation, it would be appropriate to mention that you belong to the same faith.

Before you write the letter, visit the library and consult your faculty advisers and friends to learn whatever you can about the campus. Anything you can cite that makes this job special to you would improve your chances. If a member of the faculty, even in a different department, is distinguished for work in your field, note that you would welcome the chance to know him or her. If the institution has special programs, express eagerness to participate in them. Point out that your thesis topic or your course work reflects interest in a subject related to the college's mission.

In concluding, be sure to take care of the practical matters regarding further communications. It is especially important to mention your availability for interviews at the MLA convention and other scholarly meetings and to give your holiday address.

- Follow the advice in chapter 1 about cover letters.
- Highlight your strengths.
- Mention relevant experience not appropriate for a vita.
- Avoid self-deprecation.
- Address the practical matters regarding further communications.

THE DOSSIER

As the first chapter explains, a dossier is a set of documents that constitute your credentials for employment. A dossier usually contains a curriculum vitae, letters of recommendation, and a transcript. University placement services keep the dossiers on file and send them directly to prospective employers. As soon as you decide to enter the job market, you should visit the placement office on your campus and find out about the procedures it follows and the services it offers.

In any case, you should plan to get your dossier in order as early in the school year as possible. It might be wise to set up a series of deadlines for yourself: prepare your vita by 15 August; request letters of recommendation by 31 August; have your entire dossier available for prospective employers no later than 1 October.

Curriculum Vitae

This document may be called by some other title, such as "vita," "cv," or "personal and professional information." It is the academic equivalent of a résumé, a highly condensed educational and professional biography-at-a-glance. One copy goes into your dossier. You should keep the master copy, because a photocopy must accompany every letter of application.

Your placement office may have a standard form. You should probably not use it. It is likely to be geared toward undergraduate and nonacademic employment, or else it will be too general for your purposes. Furthermore, you will have to update it regularly for the rest of your academic career, and you would do better to adopt the customary practice of writing your own from the beginning. Follow the instructions in this section, and refer to the model vitas in appendix C for guidance.

Make sure that it is neat and attractively formatted. It should not be excessively long; three or four pages are an absolute maximum, one or two are preferable. The typing should be of professional quality, and you should use the best-quality photocopying—under no circumstances should you use dittos. Your vita is an ideal use for word processing; not only can you produce letter-perfect copy, but also you can update it constantly.

The vita should begin with basic personal information: name, addresses, telephone numbers. You are easier to reach if you give your home as well as any departmental or business addresses and telephone numbers. Information on age, marital status, number of children, health, ethnic or national origin, and religious affiliation is sometimes found in a vita. It is inappropriate, and indeed in most instances illegal, for potential employers to ask candidates for such information. It is not illegal for the candidate to volunteer it, and if, in your judgment, factors crucial to your qualifications or to your eventual decision are involved, then you may want to include the relevant items. Obviously, however, if most candidates provide such information as a matter of course, the purpose of the policies and laws—to prevent unfair discrimination—will be frustrated. Therefore many individuals and groups in the profession, including the MLA Commission on the Status of Women, strongly urge all candidates to omit any mention of these items from their vitas. You should at least be aware of your right to withhold the information and of the reasons why this right was established.

Next list your educational background, beginning with the most recent level and ending with your first postsecondary institution. Include the names of institutions attended, dates, degrees earned, field of study, and titles of theses or dissertations. Give an account of your progress toward the PhD if you have not yet completed it. You may include a partial list of courses taken, especially if you have developed a second area of expertise.

Next, if applicable, list any academic honors or prizes; do not, however, include irrelevant nonacademic awards. In general, limit the list to postsecondary or higher education; only exceptional achievements from high school might be mentioned.

After the awards, describe your teaching experience. Give descriptive titles of the courses, the institution where you taught, and the extent of your experience, including the number of sections and quarters, semesters, or years. If you have a great deal of experience, limit the list to the items closest to the job you hope to get. After your experience, list the areas of teaching interest. As most employers prefer a candidate with some flexibility, it is to your advantage to list several different interests, but they must be backed up with either experience or educational preparation.

You may list other employment experience if it relates to the job. For example, work as a research assistant, editor, or librarian might be relevant for positions in research-oriented institutions; work as a student counselor or club adviser might be relevant for institutions that stress teaching.

Next you should list publications and, separately, conference papers and lectures. These categories give evidence of your entry into full professional status; see the previous chapter for advice on how to generate some items for these sections. Here again, use your judgment about what you list. If you are interested in teaching creative writing, you should probably include the poems you published in your college literary magazine; otherwise, omit them and include only scholarly and critical articles. You should also include here your work in progress: manuscripts completed and submitted but not yet accepted, large projects with partially completed drafts, or research well under way. In every case, you must be ready to show what you have done and discuss in detail what you are working on; do not put down ideas you hope to work on later. If you have completed your thesis, you ought to have something under way, either a revision of the thesis for publication or a new project. To have no work in progress will seem unimaginative.

Next list your academic service, that is, work you have done on departmental committees, organizing conferences, working on a journal, and so on. You should include only items that involved some sort of formal appointment, election, or recognition.

Most vitas include a list of foreign languages in which the candidate has some proficiency. For foreign language teachers, this section is essential. Mention each language, followed by a description of your skills: for example, "near-native command," "fluent speaking ability," "reading knowledge."

Toward the end, you may insert a miscellaneous or special category. Foreign language teachers might mention residence abroad. If you have mentioned an interest in teaching an interdisciplinary field, such as literature and music, you might want to cite significant ability and experience as a musician here.

Next name the professional organizations of which you are a member. These memberships provide evidence of commitment to the profession and awareness of its activities. Since joining requires nothing more than filling out a form and paying the dues, it is foolish not to belong to the major associations. All of them give their members useful services. A typical list ought to include the MLA, a regional MLA, the appropriate teacher-oriented organization (such as the NCTE and AATs), and the societies organized around the subject(s) that you teach and study.

Early in your career, you will probably receive in the mail an invitation to be listed in various directories, such as the *Directory of American Scholars*. You need not buy the directory, but you should send in the form and have your name listed. Some scholars include the names of directories where they are listed along with association memberships. No honor or distinction is conferred by the invitations or the listings, but they help identify you to your colleagues and establish your reputation in the profession.

Finally, you should list the names and addresses of three or four senior members of the profession who have agreed to write letters of recommendation for you. See the next section for more advice on obtaining letters of recommendation.

18

In the early stages of your career, the last item on the vita should be the address of the office where your dossier is available.

The Transcript

The transcript, an official record of your courses and grades, is usually but not always included in the dossier. At most schools, you have to pay a fee every time the dossier goes out with an official copy of the transcript, and many universities will not allow an unofficial (sealless) copy of the transcript to be included in a dossier. If the charge for including the transcript seems too high, you should be sure that information about your classwork is included—for example, ask your graduate adviser to mention it in a letter. You should also say in your letters of application that the transcript will be supplied if requested, and you should be prepared to pay for it.

- Do not use a printed form for your vita; design your own, adapting models such as those in appendix C.
- Type and copy the vita neatly.
- Include all essential data.
- Do not pad the vita with irrelevant or inaccurate items.
- Include a transcript in your dossier, or be prepared to provide one.

LETTERS OF RECOMMENDATION

Whom to Ask

Several factors must be balanced in selecting the people you will ask to write your letters of recommendation. First of all, they must know you and your work thoroughly and think highly of you. Second, they must carry some authority with the people who will read the letter. Third, they should cover as much of the range of your interests as possible. Finally, they should reflect a certain professional diversity themselves. You should have at least four strong supporters willing to write for you; as noted earlier, if you cannot think of four, either you are starting the job hunt prematurely or else you should consider whether you have made a wise choice of careers.

You must have earned the support of your references well before you assemble your dossier. Take this fact into account as you plan your course of study. If you hope to have a letter from a particular member of the faculty, be sure to take that professor's classes and to make an extra effort. Think of this also from the reverse perspective: if you intend to list an interest in a field and do not have a letter from the person who teaches it, prospective employers may wonder why. If you want to call on one of your undergraduate teachers, be sure to maintain your contacts so that the letter can be based on recent information.

In general, if you are going on the job market for the first time, you will probably ask your thesis adviser and other professors who have given you good grades. If you have taught, you should ask the course supervisors to write for you. If you have any other professional accomplishments or experience, it is probably a good idea to ask the person who directed the program or evaluated your work. You should make an effort as a student to establish this kind of professional contact, so that not all your references come from classroom situations.

Consult your adviser in selecting referees, and be guided by the advice you receive. Your adviser may know that certain professors habitually write short, vague, unimpressive recommendations, that a professor who gave you a good grade nevertheless does not have a good opinion of you, or that a professor has a poor reputation among his or her colleagues. As mentioned earlier, be sensitive to any sign that someone you ask is reluctant to write for you.

Students usually overestimate the value of letters from famous scholars. Widely recognized names carry a certain authority, but such scholars are often asked to write in support of many candidates. If you are well known and sure of strong support, then of course the famous person's prestige will be useful to you. Otherwise, however, you would gain more from asking a less celebrated colleague who knows you better and will spend more time and effort on your letter. A knowledgeable, detailed letter from an assistant professor will make a stronger impression than a cursory string of platitudes from a full professor with a named chair.

If you are no longer in graduate school, you should begin to replace some of your earlier references with colleagues you have met through your professional activities. Employers evaluate not only the contents of the letters and the standing of the authors but also the implications of the particular range of referees. It is a bad sign if you have been in the profession for several years and must still rely on your former teachers for all your support.

Likewise, you ought to consider the perspective of your possible employers. If your recommendations all come from scholars known largely for their research and publications, an institution emphasizing teaching may not be favorably impressed. If you are a candidate for a position in a college where women's education has a high priority, your chances may be hurt if you have asked only men to write for you. Common sense should be your guide, but many candidates apparently fail to think at all about how their dossiers will look to potential employers.

In summary, you should try to choose four or five references who know you well, who have a high opinion of you, who cover the range of your abilities and experience, who will carry authority with outsiders, and who represent your professional interests well.

How to Proceed

When you have identified the people you want to ask, you should then get in touch with them personally. If they live too far away for you to visit their offices, then telephone. Do not under any circumstances give someone's name without asking permission. That is both discourteous and dangerous.

You should give each one a copy of your vita, offprints of any articles you have published, and a copy of your dissertation proposal. Tell them why you have asked them: because they taught a particular field you want to stress, because they supervised your teaching, because they are familiar with your work on a committee, and so on. That information will help them orient their letters toward the subjects that will help you the most.

Tell them also what kinds of jobs you are applying for and what your general plans are. Keep them informed of your progress; if you get a favorable response, such as a request for your dossier or an invitation to an interview, let them know, because they may be able to follow up the general letter with a personal contact or give you useful tips.

It may be helpful to give recommenders additional information about yourself, beyond what is on the vita and what they already know. Personal touches in a letter of recommendation add to its impact.

If you are requesting letters for a dossier, the placement office may give you a form.

Such forms usually include a waiver of your right to see the contents of the letter. Whether to sign it must be your decision; see chapter 1, pages 4–5, for a discussion of the pros and cons.

You should always supply the recommender with a stamped, addressed envelope. This simple courtesy increases the likelihood that the letter will be written and filed in your dossier on time. Mention to the recommenders what your deadline is, and allow plenty of time for them to write. Six weeks is by no means too long. A couple of weeks before you need to have the completed dossier, check with the placement office to be sure the letters have come in; if not, you should tactfully remind the procrastinators that the deadline is near.

Don't forget that letters are sometimes lost in the mail; remind everyone you ask to keep a carbon or photocopy. Most faculty members will keep a copy on file as a matter of course. As you advance in the profession, you should do the same. The copies are particularly useful when you want to write a new letter for the same person. As with the vita, a word processor is extremely useful for composing, filing, revising, updating, and reformatting letters of recommendation.

Finally, if you continue to use your dossier for several years, you should replace the old letters of recommendation every three or four years. You may want to ask some of the same people to write for you again. If so, you should keep them constantly up to date on your professional development: send them offprints; write, call, or visit occasionally; try to see them at professional meetings; invite them to come hear your papers; and give them an updated vita when you ask for the new letter.

Meanwhile, however, you should be making new contacts and finding new mentors. They might include the chair of the department you teach in, a senior member of the department who is in your field, a senior colleague who knows your teaching, the organizer of a conference session where you spoke, the editor of a journal that published your article, or simply an important person in your field with whom you have established a professional relation. For more advice on developing contacts, joining networks, and finding mentors, see the section on conventions, pages 9–11.

Updating the Dossier

Periodically, you should consider updating your dossier. Generally speaking, placement services simply add new material as it comes to them but never remove anything without specific authorization. You should begin therefore by getting in touch with the placement office to find out what is in your dossier. Inquire about procedures for removing material; you may need to get permission to have letters of recommendation taken out. You should therefore begin during the summer, so as to allow enough time.

Your vita should be replaced every year, if possible, to reflect your growing list of accomplishments and professional experience. While you could simply add a new page for each year, the vita will look more professional and create a more favorable impression if you revise it completely.

Letters of recommendation should also be replaced periodically, about every three years. You may obtain letters from new recommenders without removing the old ones at any time. Old letters, however favorable, often give an impression that conflicts with your later development. At best, they will omit any mention of the important work you have done since they were written. To obtain a new set of letters, you should follow the same procedures outlined for the original set.

Check to be sure that the placement office has updated your dossier as you requested. Most placement offices are understaffed and work under great pressure at certain times of the year. Complete the removal of the old material before you begin assembling the new dossier; otherwise you may discover that the new material was inadvertently removed at the same time.

- Get letters of recommendation from people who know you well.
- Begin lining up references well in advance.
- Consult your adviser about whom to ask.
- Select references so as to cover all your major qualifications.
- Keep in mind the perspective of potential employers.
- Ask personally whether a person will agree to recommend you.
- Keep your references informed about your work and your job search.
- Give references a stamped, addressed envelope.
- Check with the placement office to be sure the dossier is complete.
- Update your dossier periodically to reflect your new accomplishments.

INTERVIEWS: BEFOREHAND

Scheduling

Being invited for an interview means that you have survived the first screening of the applicants. For the hiring department, interviews involve a considerable expense of time, effort, and sometimes money. Normally you will not be invited unless you have a real chance at the job. Many interviews for faculty jobs in language and literature are conducted at the MLA convention in December.

As a rule, departments that want to interview candidates schedule the interviews ahead of time. If you have not heard from any of the schools that requested your dossier, you should call early in December before the semester ends to ask about your status. Few interview appointments are arranged at the convention itself, and you should not go expecting to arrange them on the spot. If you have several interviews to schedule, try to allow at least an hour between them; you may have to travel between hotels, and although the distances are not great, the interviewers may fall behind their schedules, the elevators may be delayed by the crowds, and you will need some time to collect your thoughts.

When the interviewer sets the appointment, he or she will probably be able to tell you in what hotel the meeting will take place, but not the room number, if it is to be in a suite. As soon as you arrive at the convention, begin calling to confirm the appointments and to obtain the room numbers. Most hotel switchboards will not give out room numbers but will put your call through or take a message. Since the lines are swamped with calls during the convention and the people you want to reach are not always there, you must allow for some frustrating delays. In short, locate the people you are supposed to see the first thing on arrival. If you wait until the last minute, you may find yourself standing in line for a phone as the hour for your interview passes.

Many interviews take place in the Job Information Center, and the MLA encourages all interviewers to register their room numbers there as well. Occasionally an interviewer may not even be in the scheduled hotel; in such cases, a message will almost certainly be left at the Job Information Center. If you are unable to locate someone through the hotel operators, check with the Job Information Center first. Besides helping with communications, it is staffed by MLA personnel who can answer questions and help you with problems. The interviews that take place there are conducted in a large room with dozens of small tables; staff members escort the candidates to the right place at the right time.

Other interviews will take place in the hotel rooms, anything from an ordinary single to a large suite. You may find yourself alone with the department chair or facing a roomful of interviewers. The fewer there are, the more likely they are to be senior members of the department. If you have the chance ahead of time, you should feel free to ask about the conditions of the interview, including who will be there, but the department chair may not know until the last minute. Styles of interviewing vary greatly; some people will try to put you at ease and help you show your best side, while others will deliberately subject you to some stressful questioning.

Some questions come up in almost all interviews. You will be asked about your dissertation or, if you have already finished your doctorate, about your current research. You will be asked about your teaching experience, methods, and preferences and will have an opportunity to ask some questions.

In general, interviews are meant to give potential employers a sense of the candidates' personal qualities. The interviewers will obviously be interested in your intelligence, your manner, your poise, your sense of humor, and similar qualities. Not all interviewers know what they are looking for, however, or what is the best way to find it. Unfortunately, a few interviews may simply be pro forma, because the department has already decided to offer the job to someone else. Occasionally a team of interviewers will spend more time talking to one another, maybe even arguing with one another, than talking to you. Don't be surprised at anything.

The interview will usually be scheduled for a fixed amount of time, probably a half hour or an hour. Be sure to make all the important points about your qualifications and to ask all the questions you need to ask before the time gets short. At the end, if the interviewer does not volunteer the information, ask about what will happen next, when you will hear whether you are still under consideration, and if so, whether there will be a campus visit, for example.

Preparation

The general preparation for an interview consists of going over your own ideas with a little common sense. You can count on being asked about your thesis or your research; prepare some answers to questions about it. Be ready to give a succinct description and also to elaborate. Be able to describe in detail what you have completed and to outline your plans for the next steps. Pick out the most interesting and original aspects, as well as those you know best, and work up brief explanations.

Go over your teaching experience and expectations in the same way. Have prompt responses to questions about how you teach, or would teach, and about what you want to teach. Think of some important classes you have given, and be ready to describe them or to tell what made them work. Look for ways to show that you have been successful as a teacher. Be well informed about the program in your department: how it is structured, what the requirements are, what methods are used. Know the names of the textbooks you use.

Besides taking stock of your own record, think about your career and the profession in general. Peruse the journals of some professional associations in your field; it would be better still to be a member. Reflect on the broad questions relating to your field, such as why students need to study foreign languages or what is the value of literature. Be aware of the current controversies and problems of the profession, and venture some tentative opinions. Consider your own ambitions and what you would like to be doing in ten or twenty years.

The best way to get ready for interviews is to practice. If your department does not hold mock interviews, get a group of your fellow students together and interview one another. It will be as useful to pose questions as to respond to them. You will develop a sense of what interviewers are likely to want to know, and you will have a chance to rehearse your answers. If you are caught unawares or if you blurt out a poor answer, it won't matter in a mock interview, and you will be less likely to repeat your mistake when it counts. After you've practiced, discuss your impressions.

When you know who is going to interview you, you should do some specific preparation. Go to the library and find out all you can about the school and the department. Be prepared to talk about specific characteristics—small or large, urban or rural, public or private, special mission, unusual programs or facilities. Ask your professors and friends if they know anything about the school. Women and minority candidates will find it useful to know ahead of time what the school's record on affirmative action has been, whether there are ethnic and women's studies programs, what the makeup of the student body is.

Make a particular effort to find out who the senior members of the department are and who is in your field. Nothing will hurt you more in an interview than to reveal that you have not heard of someone who is locally considered important or who has done work in your field.

Attitude

Dress up a little for your interviews. Men should wear a jacket and tie and have their hair, beard, and mustache reasonably well trimmed and groomed. Women should wear a skirt and jacket. Dress for a businesslike effect, not for a party. Academics generally dress somewhat more casually than Wall Street bankers, however; a dark suit may be overdoing it.

Keep in mind that the interview is a reciprocal exchange, not an oral exam. You want to learn about your potential future colleagues as well as give them the chance to learn about you. You should take seriously the possibility that you would not like the job and should try to observe and listen carefully. This attitude will help increase your real and apparent self-confidence, and the information you gather will be useful if, as may happen, you have to choose among several offers. Never forget that there are good jobs outside the academic world; if the only jobs you find in teaching do not seem suitable for you, do not hesitate to look elsewhere.

As explained in chapter 1, by the time you leave graduate school and accept a job, you should have made the transition from thinking like a student to thinking like a professional. You have exceptional ability, extensive training, and highly desirable skills; you know how to do something important, you can do it well and professionally, and you should be able to make a living doing it. Don't let the difficult job market erode that sense of yourself as a professional. You may have to temporize, compromise, postpone some expectations, and reconsider some options, but you should not despair. You do not have to take whatever is offered or put up with mistreatment. Your chances of success will in fact be better if your manner conveys the confidence that you have other choices, that you are not powerless, that you consider yourself a colleague of the person(s) conducting the interview and expect to be treated as such.

Maintaining your self-assurance through the period of job hunting is bound to be difficult. The hierarchical structure of graduate programs and the grim job market take a toll on almost all candidates. The problem is compounded for those confronting prejudices based on sex, race, class, sexual preference, physical disability, age, or institution. Your resiliency will make you feel better and will make you a better prospect. To develop it, you should prepare well, practice in advance, and know what to expect.

Avoid thinking of the interview as a test you have to pass. In one way, that is a relief: there are no right answers to the questions. Usually interviewers do not waste their time checking on your scholarly competence by asking specific questions about your research; they can find out more from reading your dissertation or sample chapter and from analyzing your dossier. If the discussion begins to feel like an oral exam, you probably ought to change the direction of the interview; make your reply succinct, and try to lead into a question of your own: "That is a very interesting area; will there be an opportunity for me to teach a course on it?" or "I would like to do some further research on that; could you tell me something about your library facilities (or research support)?" In an interview as in the classroom, it is better simply to acknowledge that you don't know some things.

In another way, however, a test may seem more pleasant than an interview: everyone who does well on a test passes, but most interviews can lead to only one job offer. For that reason it is especially important to think of the interview as a professional exchange. You may profit from it even if you do not get the specific job. The interviewers may have influence in other areas of the profession; they may recommend you to participate in a conference, to review a book, to be a candidate for another job. A year later, some of them may be at other institutions and put your name in for a job there. In other words, you succeeded in the interview if you impressed the interviewers as a promising candidate, whether or not you got a job offer.

An interview consists of personal interactions. No two are alike, and you have to trust your own sensitivity to gauge the way things are going and to adjust your role accordingly. At first, the interviewers should be in control. They will ask the first questions and establish a sort of agenda. You have your own agenda, however, and you should be sure to make room for it in the time available. Part of what you must demonstrate is your ability to seize the initiative in this kind of situation and to impose your own sense of priorities to some degree. A delicate balance must be struck; you do not want to seem passive but you also do not want to monopolize the time. If this advice sounds like a double bind, remember that you need the same skills to teach a good seminar, to serve on a committee, to appear on a panel, or to interview a candidate. You have many chances to practice ahead of time, and you will be using these skills for your whole academic career.

By the same token, you should be more concerned to earn the respect of the interviewer than to be liked. Actually, people usually learn to like someone they respect, but liking someone is never a sufficient reason to make a job offer. Put yourself in the interviewer's place, and ask yourself the following questions: "Can I explain to the dean why my department wants to hire this person?" and "Would this person represent my department's interests well on the curriculum committee?" You would like to give the impression that the department will be making a mistake if they let you get away, because you are going to make a mark in the profession.

You must not be shy. If you think of yourself as a shy person, sign up immediately for a course to help you deal with it. Many signs of shyness can be overcome easily. Feel free to think for a while before you respond to a question. Don't speak overeagerly or too fast. Try to keep the volume relatively high and the pitch relatively low. Speak in complete sentences, and do not end declarative statements with an interrogative tone.

- Arrange your schedule of appointments early.
- Prepare ahead of time and practice.
- Know all you can about your prospective employers.
- Make a good appearance.
- Act like a colleague.
- Assert yourself at appropriate times.
- Think of the interview as a professional exchange, not a test.

INTERVIEWS: DURING AND AFTER

Questions and Answers

In all the exchanges during an interview, you must strike some kind of compromise between giving the most pleasing impression and giving the most truthful or accurate impression. The ideal situation, of course, is a job for which you are the perfect candidate, just as you are. Such jobs are rare, however, and even for them you should be concerned to present your perfect qualifications in the most effective manner. For most academic positions, the best candidates seem to combine intelligence, congeniality, awareness, adaptability, and commitment both to teaching and to research. For some positions, though, either teaching or research may take priority, and some candidates find only certain fields or certain activities interesting. You should not present a false picture of yourself, promise to teach courses, or commit yourself to producing research if you do not intend to do what you say. Nothing that follows should be construed as a recommendation to lie.

Respond as positively as possible to all questions, and phrase your own questions in a positive way. In particular, do not denigrate your own thesis, the courses you have taught, or your department. Avoid such lines as "I'm limiting my study to . . ."; "It's a very minor work, but no one has ever studied it before, so I . . ."; "I've never had a chance to teach anything except composition . . ."; "The department was pretty weak in that area . . ."; "The person who teaches that is not very good so I didn't take it . . . ." In every area, emphasize the value of what you have done and your intention of building on that base.

As a junior member of the department, you will almost certainly be given a lot of teaching responsibilities in the lowest-level courses, such as elementary language and English composition. You must therefore be careful not to disparage them. You may find that the interviewers have no interest in talking about them; if so, do not force the subject. If they show some interest, be ready to discuss methods. Ask questions about the way they conduct the courses: At what level is literature introduced? Is there a language lab? a writing center? Is writing taught across the curriculum? Is language achievement measured by proficiency tests?

26

Interviewers often ask, "What course would you like to teach?" Be sure to have an idea appropriate for the level you might be asked to teach; your inquiries beforehand about the school should be helpful. Specify in answering that you are talking about a freshman- or sophomore-level course, or an advanced elective, or a course for majors, or a course on foreign literature in translation for business majors, and so forth. As the interviewer may ask you for a course at a certain level, it would be well to have thought in advance about a range of courses. The courses you propose should be related to your own research and preparation and should be realistic in conception. Discuss them with your adviser before you present them in an interview.

If you have to introduce the subject of teaching, give your questions a positive cast. Don't ask, "What will I have to teach?" or "How much comp will I have to teach?" Instead ask, "Would I have an opportunity to teach a course on . . . ?" Don't ask, "Is there a lot of advising?" Say, "Tell me about student-faculty contacts outside the classroom." If the interviewer brings up an unusual or challenging situation, try to respond to it as an opportunity. In a real interview, candidates were asked, "How do you feel about teaching in a women's college?" Everyone who answered, "I wouldn't mind," was dropped off the list.

In discussing your research, you should be prepared for whatever depth of questioning the interviewers may have in mind. Some will be satisfied with a brief statement of the main thesis; others will want a chapter-by-chapter analysis. You should have a plan to revise for publication whatever you are working on. You need not feel bound to follow the plan if your work takes a different course or if you devise a different plan later; but even if no one ever asks you about it, you ought to be thinking about how to publish your scholarly work in the most advantageous way. Likewise, you should have in mind some further projects that you will want to undertake when the current one is completed. The best ones will seem to have grown out of your present work.

For any department that is interested in your research, you ought to ask some questions about the institutional support for scholarly work. Ask about such things as library holdings in your field, secretarial support for typing manuscripts, travel funds for confer-.ences, grants for research projects, fellowships and leaves, and so forth. Your interest will create a good impression, and the information may prove useful in deciding whether the offer is a good one.

You should also ask about the practical matters relating to the job. You should have no hesitation about asking what your salary would be, what the course load is, what the term of the contract is, how decisions are made about renewal and promotion, what the principal fringe benefits are, and so forth. These are normal concerns; the interviewer may not be able to answer all your questions precisely, but he or she should be willing to discuss them candidly. If you find the answers evasive, proceed with caution.

Special Situations

Large departments often appoint hiring committees, and candidates may find themselves being interviewed by many people, not just a department chair. Such group interviews place extra burdens on the candidate. You must not direct all your responses to the senior people present; usually everyone on the committee has a vote. The relations among the questioners may tell you a great deal about the department: Do they make sure everyone has a chance to ask something? Do they seem to react similarly to your responses? Or do you detect signs of conflict among them? You may even find that they ignore you and talk among themselves. With so little time and so little knowledge of the group, you have almost no hope of influencing the group's dynamics. Try to be attentive and courteous to everyone. If things seem to be out of control, try to remain calm; it is not your fault.

Almost all academic interviewers will try to give you the best opportunity to show your strengths. They will try to put you at ease, because they want to know what you will be like under normal circumstances. You may, however, encounter someone who believes in stress interviews; if so, life in that department will probably also subject you to a lot of stress. A stress interview may involve hostile questions, or it may involve putting you in an uncomfortable position. Of course, some stress is inevitable, and some stressful questions and situations may be unintentional. In any case, you cannot foresee them, and the best advice is to react with as much poise and self-assurance as you can muster. Stay aware of your own feelings. If you are being bullied, you may decide to fight back, to roll with the punches, or to walk out; whatever you choose to do, try to maintain your own dignity.

At the other extreme, you may conclude that the interviewer has no real interest in you at all. There could be several reasons. Between the times when your interview was set up and when it took place, another candidate may have been chosen. There may have been an inside or favored candidate all along. If you are a woman or a member of a minority group, you may have been interviewed only because of affirmative action pressure. Whatever the reason, you should probably ignore it and carry out your end as professionally as possible. An interview is always a professional exchange of some kind; even though you may feel that you have been brought in under false pretenses, you should still take advantage of the chance to make a good impression on the interviewers. The inside candidate may go somewhere else, another job may open up, the interviewer may remember you on another occasion; you should keep those possibilities open, however slim they are. You have nothing whatsoever to gain by expressing anger or bitterness in this situation. At a minimum, you can treat it as a practice interview and try out approaches that might seem too risky if you thought you were a serious candidate.

Interviewers who make sexist remarks or, worse still, who use the situation for sexual harassment pose a different problem. The MLA Commission on the Status of Women has received a number of reports of sexist comments and some of sexual harassment. Each candidate has to decide on her or his own response to such a situation. To let it pass establishes your role in an undesirable way; to challenge it may mean losing a good job, although not always. To react strongly—by walking out, for example—increases the likelihood of permanent bad relations with that individual and probably with the department, but only you can judge whether you are willing to accept that outcome and whether the offense warrants it. You may also consider writing to the offender's dean or president or making some kind of public accusation. Talk it over with a close friend and with a support group of some kind before you act. You may be justified, and your action may help others in the long run; but it may also involve you in a drawn-out and painful conflict, and it may hurt you as much as the guilty party. Only you can decide what to do, but others can give you useful advice and moral support.

Members of various groups—ethnic minorities, the physically challenged, older candidates, for example—may encounter subtle and not-so-subtle signals that they are unwelcome. "It's a good place to bring up a family" may mean "Gays are not welcome." "There's a lot of snow" may mean "Your wheelchair makes me uneasy." "It's very rural" may mean "I don't think blacks/Jews/Hispanics would fit in." Sometimes the interviewer may be trying to give you a realistic appraisal of the situation; at other times, it may be a thinly veiled attempt to discourage you. If you are in such a group, you have no doubt experienced the problem already and thought about the possible ways to handle it. You may want to bring the subject into the open and discuss it frankly, or you may decide that you would prefer not to have such a person as a colleague, much less as chair of your department. Here again, only you can assess the situation, and only you can decide what response is right for you.

Afterward

After every interview, talk it over with friends and advisers. You should learn something from each one. Almost everyone has at least one really disastrous interview at some time; such an experience is painful to live through, but you can still profit from it. Analyze what went wrong; plan how to avoid the same thing next time. In some cases, your adviser may be able to get inside information about the impression you made. Many candidates leave interviews thinking they have done brilliantly because they talked a lot; the interviewers may have had a different opinion of the monologue. If there were questions that you answered badly, think about a better answer for the next time. In a rare case, you may be able to recover from a poor answer by writing afterward—for example, if you had not read a book you were asked about, you might salvage something by reading it right away and writing to thank the interviewer for bringing it to your attention. It's a long shot, but worth trying if the job seems right for you and if you think you did well otherwise.

- Be positive.
- Have ready answers to the obvious questions.
- Ask about the things that concern you.
- Do not become upset or angry if an interview goes badly.
- Analyze interviews afterward and learn from them.

CAMPUS VISITS

Any job interview is a sign of a department's serious interest in the candidate; an invitation to a campus visit is usually an even more favorable sign. You should therefore take whatever steps are necessary to make the trip, under most circumstances. Campus visits generally give both parties a longer and deeper look at each other, and the process entails pleasures and stresses not encountered in a brief convention interview. An invitation to a campus visit usually has less significance if there has been no previous convention interview, especially if you are asked to pay your own expenses and if the schedule suggests that you will in effect simply be interviewed. By the same token, if you have already been interviewed once, if the institution is investing some of its budget for your travel expenses, and if many people have committed time to meet you, then you probably have been shortlisted—that is, kept on the list of the two or three top candidates. It is therefore worth your while to make every effort to capitalize on the opportunity.

The visit will likely be arranged by a telephone call from the chair to you; if the invitation comes by letter, telephone to accept and to work out the arrangements. You ought to ask about several practical matters: who will pay the expenses and, if the department is paying, what exactly it will pay for. In some places, it is not legal for state-supported institutions to spend money for candidates' travel; in such a case, you would be wise to invest the money yourself, unless you have no interest in the job or already have another offer you prefer. Other possible arrangements are that the department will pay a fixed sum, which is less than the total cost of the trip, or that it will pay for transportation but not for meals, and so forth. The important thing is to know in advance what to expect. You should also ask when you would receive reimbursement, if it matters; in some cases, two or three months may elapse between your visit and the arrival of your check.

You should also ask about the schedule for your visit. Campus visits may be handled in many different ways. Some departments prefer to have candidates go through a series of one-on-one interviews with many different people. Others conduct a group interview. You should feel free to ask who will meet with you and in what context. A dean or other administrator may talk to you, and it is not unheard of for student representatives and even department secretaries to hold a formal interview with job candidates.

Frequently, the candidate is asked to give an informal talk or a full lecture or to teach a class. If you have been following the advice in the previous sections of this guide, you know that you should have suitable topics ready to suggest in case such a request is made. If you do not, select one as soon as possible. Be sure to get clear instructions about what to do; know how long you will have to speak and to what audience. If you are to teach a class, ask how many students there will be, at what level, and whether you could see a course syllabus. Normally, you will be asked to do something related to your thesis, or at least to your presumed special interests. Depending on the length of your stay, you may have morning coffee, lunch, dinner, casual drinks, a large reception, or several social events with different groups.

When you are going to a campus for a visit, some knowledge of the institution is crucial. Ask the chair to send you a catalog and whatever other documentation may be available. Read it as carefully as you can, to get a feel for the place before you get there. Learn the names of the members of the department, and try to find out something about them. Know what the school is famous for and proud of. If time is too short for the chair to send you material, do what research you can in your library and placement office. Consult your professors and fellow students, especially any who were students at the school. It may prove very helpful to know of local enthusiasms and conflicts and to know something about the personalities of the people you are likely to meet.

When you are there, be prepared for a mixed reception. At times, you will probably be treated like visiting royalty; at other times, you may feel as though you are losing an endurance contest. The campus visit is your best opportunity to find out what the job would really be like. You will be able to look at the facilities, meet some of the students, and get acquainted with your future colleagues. You can probably tell whether they get along well or quarrel, whether they seem happy or embittered, whether they have plans or recriminations uppermost in their minds. At the same time, of course, you have the chance to show them your talents and skills.

Obviously, you will do everything possible to make a good impression, but you must also be yourself. It is almost always a mistake to tailor your deeply held beliefs to please someone else. Emphasize your strong points, be tactful, be sensitive to their beliefs, but don't lie about your own ideas or give a false impression of yourself. Do not let your guard down during the social events; they may be more relaxed and casual than a lecture or interview, but your behavior will contribute to the overall impression you make. Don't let the stress of the situation or the relief of having given your lecture successfully induce

30

you to drink too much and ruin an otherwise good impression. Don't let the cordiality of the welcome raise your hopes too high, either; they are trying to woo you as much as you are trying to win the job, but they may make the offer to another candidate.

The final step, as with other interviews, is to ask what to expect next. You should not hesitate to ask whether there are other candidates, although you should not ask who they are. If someone volunteers the information, under no circumstances say anything bad about them. You may also ask for an honest assessment of your prospects. Most chairs will do their best to answer such questions forthrightly and will appreciate candor on your side – if you are being considered by another school, for example – but do not press for answers that are obviously being withheld.

- Be willing to make some sacrifices for a campus interview.
- Ask about practical arrangements in advance.
- Be prepared to give a talk or teach a class.
- Find out all you can about the campus before you go.
- Learn all you can while you are there.
- Be careful.
- Be yourself.

OFFERS

The final stage in a job hunt is receiving and accepting an offer. Most offers are made first by telephone, although they may be made by mail and even sometimes in person at the end of an interview. Candidates should be wary of offers made on the spot, especially if pressure is applied for an instantaneous response; any legitimate offer will allow the candidate a few days in which to consider the response. Usually, by the end of the search, the department chair has grown as weary of waiting as the job seekers have, while the authorization to hire has been pending in a dean's or provost's office. Once clearance is received, the department wants to get its first choice and to have time to go down the list if the first choice goes elsewhere.

Usually, therefore, the department chair or the head of the search committee, or perhaps a dean, will telephone and announce that the offer is going to be made. The actual offer is always written, and it should be signed in two copies by both the employer and the employee, each of whom keeps a copy. The telephone call is to sound out the candidate about the likelihood of acceptance and to discuss practical details. You should always express pleasure at the news, but you should avoid making a full commitment right away. Ask how soon you must respond; if you have a real reason to want more time, such as the possibility of another offer, be honest about the situation and ask for a little more time. Be reasonable, however; not only the hiring departments but other candidates will be on tenterhooks until you make up your mind.

You may want to ask about some practical aspects of the job and the details of the offer. Among the former would be such matters as teaching load, class assignments, starting dates, other responsibilities, office space, and secretarial support. These are usually not specified in the contract, and they may be subject to last-minute change according to conditions and may vary from year to year. The written offer should always specify salary, rank, benefits, term of employment, and conditions of probation for tenure (some of these items may be covered by reference to a faculty handbook or similar document).

The offer may be in the form of a letter or that of a printed contract. You should not consider yourself hired until you have received and replied to a written offer. To accept an offer, you normally return a signed copy of the document. If no copy is provided, make one for yourself.

Many candidates feel lucky to have received an offer and accept whatever terms are presented. The job market has not been conducive to bargaining; unless you have a competitive offer from another institution, you will find it difficult to insist on a higher salary or other concessions. If you are fortunate enough to have been offered more than one job, you should think carefully about all the factors. As mentioned in the beginning, your personal interests and abilities must be taken into consideration, but it is dangerous to let mere preferences rule out otherwise suitable jobs. The long-term possibilities are very important; tenure-track jobs are much scarcer than others and are generally more desirable.

Many jobs nowadays are non-tenure-track positions, either part-time or temporary. For new PhDs and ABDs, such positions can provide satisfactory employment for a few years; one can eke out an existence on the income, get teaching experience, pursue research and writing projects, and remain in close contact with academic colleagues. The conditions are not, however, suitable for a lifetime career and indeed do not support the research and independent thought that are required to qualify for tenure and to achieve success in the academic world. Professional associations and conscientious administrators regularly deplore the abuse and exploitation of part-time and temporary staff, but financial pressures have exerted a greater influence. If, after holding several jobs, you are still living on part-time and temporary teaching, it is probably time to look elsewhere. Only if you can see clear evidence that your qualifications are improving should you persist in these marginal positions.

Foreign institutions sometimes recruit American PhDs. Living and working in a different culture can be very rewarding; if the culture has some relation to your field of specialization, time spent there will become a useful credential. At the same time, you should be aware of some risks. Institutions that are actively recruiting are often in countries without a well-established system and tradition of higher education. The working conditions, rights and privileges of the faculty, and level of student preparation may differ dramatically from what you are accustomed to in the United States. The periodicals, including the *MLA Job Information Lists*, that carry advertisements from foreign schools have no way to verify the statements and promises of any advertiser, and the publication of the ads does not in any way constitute an endorsement or guarantee. Occasionally Americans and other visiting scholars report severe violations of their contracts and alarming infringements of their rights. You will not have the same avenues of recourse abroad that exist in America: professional associations, the American Association of University Professors, faculty unions, and the American judicial system. You will usually find foreign positions more difficult to investigate than domestic ones, but you should make whatever efforts you can and should recognize that some additional risks are involved.

Although it is unwise to accept an offer the moment it is made, if you are strongly inclined to accept there is no reason not to be straightforward with the chair or head of the search about your feelings and probable response. Once you have decided to accept it, you should also inform all your advisers, your references, your placement bureau, and other departments that are considering you. If your candidacy is still active somewhere else, you should telephone immediately and let them know. If they have a chance to make an offer you would prefer, you should ask about your status and when you might know their decision; be candid in explaining the situation. Whether to turn down an acceptable offer in the hope of a better one is a classic dilemma; you must decide each case on the basis of your evaluation of the job, of your goals, and of your qualifications. It would also be wise to consult your advisers. In any case, you do not have any special obligation to the first department that asks you, except to be prompt and frank in responding.

Even after you have notified other departments that you have accepted an offer and are no longer a candidate, you may receive a second and more desirable offer. Colleges and universities generally abide by the rule that no offers should be made after 1 May to faculty employed in other schools, but before 1 May the individual faculty member may in good conscience go elsewhere. It is not to anyone's advantage to have unwilling members of the faculty; if for no other reason, most departments will make no effort to hold a person who wants to be released from a contract. If you have acted in good faith throughout and you get a second offer that is clearly better for you, you should probably accept it. You will certainly disappoint the first department, and you may cost them the line. You may also therefore cost some other candidate a job. It is not a decision to be made lightly, but you cannot jeopardize your future just to be courteous. Consult your adviser before you take such a step; if you decide to do it, inform the first department as quickly and as openly as possible. Tell the second department what the situation is; they may be willing to intercede on your behalf. Pulling out of the agreement will not endear you to the first department, but if you have done it for sound professional reasons, they will understand.

- Take time to consider an offer before you accept it.
- Clarify all the details.
- After a few years, you should reconsider your career plans if your only offers are temporary or part-time jobs.
- Inform those who need to know as soon as you accept an offer.
- Do not consider yourself hired without a written offer.

TO THOSE ALREADY EMPLOYED AS FULL-TIME FACULTY MEMBERS

Most of the preceding advice on job seeking will seem familiar, perhaps boringly or depressingly so, to those who have already begun a full-time position. When you have found your first job, you have cause to celebrate and congratulate yourself. You have passed one of the most difficult professional competitions in our society, after having completed one of the most demanding educational programs. You now have the responsibility, the challenge, and the joy of communicating to your students the love of literature and language that attracted you to the discipline in the beginning. You share in the privileges and pleasures of the academic life.

You must not suppose, however, that job hunting is an ordeal that you complete once and for all and then forget. Most junior faculty nowadays teach at more than one institution before obtaining a tenured appointment. In effect they remain on the job market throughout the probationary period of six or more years. A few additional suggestions may be useful for job seekers or possible job seekers already employed full-time.

1. The dossier. It is obviously of central importance to keep your dossier current. If you have had only a few years of experience, you will probably want to keep the old dossier, updating it each year. If you have had full-time academic employment beyond the PhD for more than three years, however, it is doubtful whether your old dossier, which represents you as a student, will still be useful. Prospective employers will be primarily interested in what you have done on your own since the PhD.

If you have moved from one institution to another, make sure that you have a letter from each one. Discuss the letters with the people you ask to write for you; they should make it clear that you were let go for reasons beyond your control, typically because the appointment was for a non-tenure-track position or because the institution imposed cutbacks on the department. Remember that your dossier is kept at your graduate institution. You may be able to add new letters to it; if not, you may be able to build a new dossier at the institution where you are employed. If you move several times, however, starting a new dossier each time will not be satisfactory, and it is preferable to ask your new references to send their letters directly to the hiring department. In any case, you will have to check into this ahead of time and be explicit in requesting your sponsors to write.

2. New letters. You should normally have a letter from the chair of each department where you have worked, especially the current one; the lack of letters from the chairs would be noticeable and peculiar. Also helpful would be letters from a course supervisor, a department member with whom you did substantive committee work, colleagues at other institutions who know your work in professional associations and meetings, and close friends in the department if they know your work well. If you have good letters of student evaluation, you may include some. If you have a book or article published, accepted, or under consideration, you may be able to use the readers' reports or ask the readers to write for you.

These letters should not be general letters of recommendation but should speak with some authority about a particular aspect of your professional activity. Your present chair may be able to go over your old dossier, helping you remove weak or obsolete letters. Since this may require the permission of the recommender, make your request diplomatically. If removal is not possible, a new letter may counteract the effects of the old one, or you may find it advisable to stop using your dossier and to rely on letters sent directly to prospective employers. Maintain contacts with professors and mentors whom you plan to ask again: send them copies of anything you write, and keep them informed about your other professional activities. Most will be happy to write new letters and send them directly to a department chair rather than to the placement office.

Whomever you ask, you must make the request directly and personally—preferably in person or by telephone, at least by letter. You should repeat your request even to those who have written for you in the past. You may ask for general permission to give someone's name as a reference during a given period, although you stand to benefit from telling your recommenders specifically what institutions you apply to. You must be sensitive to any sign of reluctance and must not press for consent. Under no circumstances should you give someone's name as a reference without asking for permission.

3. Letters of application. In applying for a new position, indicate why you are not being kept on at your present job. As mentioned above, the usual reason is that the job was defined as temporary, "on a nontenure line," or else that the institution has imposed cutbacks on the department. Some departments are known to have many more junior faculty than they can hope to promote to tenure; if you are turned down, consult the chair about how to describe your situation. Usually the reason will be that your field was already covered by a senior person. It is important in any case that you and the chair give the same reason in your letters.

In your letter, concentrate on your experience as a full-time faculty member. Mention any articles, monographs, or books published, accepted, or in circulation; full data can go in your vita. Discuss your research or writing in progress. Describe your teaching experience, doing whatever you can to indicate the quality of your work—for example, by alluding to student or peer evaluations. Mention any new courses you have devised or innovations you have introduced; the full list of courses taught will be part of your vita. Discuss important committee work, inside the institution or in professional organizations outside; once again, the list of appointments can go in the vita. Mention the kinds of student counseling or advising you have done, including individual-study courses, theses, and examination committees.

As with letters for first-time job seekers, you should write each letter individually, with the addressee in mind, emphasizing the qualities and experience that will be most useful to the prospective employer. Do not pad the letter or your vita with trivia, but do not omit any relevant parts of your professional experience. A recruiting department will be looking for a combination of past achievement and future promise. You must give persuasive evidence that you have grown and have developed new ideas since you left graduate school.

The same activities and qualities that will be useful in looking for a new job are the ones most likely to earn you reappointment, promotion, and tenure where you are now. Graduate students must exercise initiative in getting experience outside the classroom; junior faculty must even more actively build up their own credentials. All new members of the profession should seek challenges, learn new skills, develop networks, and make their work known to their peers.

In beginning a new job, it is crucial to consult the department chair about the criteria for reappointment and promotion, about the procedures for evaluation, and about your chances. Follow this interview with regular consultations to review your progress and present situation. Be guided, of course, by the local situation; a busy chair may delegate some of this counseling to another senior colleague, such as the chair of the personnel committee or the director of undergraduate studies. Many departments have a formal procedure in place for periodic evaluation and consultation with junior faculty. If yours does not, take the responsibility yourself for meeting the chair each semester for a serious analysis of your work and your prospects.

Different institutions assign different weights to the various parts of the job. Find out about these priorities early, and plan your activities accordingly. The profession has been much criticized for giving too high a priority to publication and too low a priority to effective teaching; everyone knows the phrase "Publish or perish." There is some validity to the criticism, but most institutions do in fact consider teaching, professional activity, institutional service, and public service when evaluating candidates for promotion. You must realize, however, that you will be judged on what is most important to the institution, not what is most important to you.

Publication and some forms of professional activity have the advantage that they become known to members of the profession as a matter of course. If you publish in a journal or give a paper at a conference, your name is printed and your peers will see it. Some of your colleagues will hear your papers, and any who want to can read your publications and form a reliable (to them, anyway) opinion of your ability as a scholar and a critic. Largely for this reason, publishing and professional activity are usually more valuable in job hunting than teaching experience and other forms of service are. If you publish, do not be shy about sending copies to senior colleagues in your department, your former professors, and people you have met in the same field.

If your interest and ability are directed more toward teaching or other forms of service, you should make vigorous efforts to document your excellence in these fields. Be sure that students provide trustworthy written evaluations and that peers regularly observe your classes. Join the professional organizations that focus on teaching, and take an active part in their activities. Write about the successful innovations you bring to your classes and publish the papers in appropriate journals. Make your ability available outside the classroom by giving public lectures or organizing open seminars. Get to know other dedicated teachers on the campus, and discuss professional matters with them; try to find someone who can write a convincing letter of recommendation about your teaching. All too often, years of outstanding work as a teacher show up in a dossier as no more than a list of courses taught; unfortunately, years of abominable work as a teacher look exactly the same. If teaching is your strength, you would be well advised to devote a lot of effort and ingenuity to producing convincing evidence of your excellence.

Public service, departmental administration, committee work, advising, and so on all present the same sort of difficulty as credentials. In most institutions, they are clearly ranked after teaching and scholarship but are regarded as valuable contributions. If you count on such activities to help you get reappointed, promoted, or hired elsewhere, you must find ways to document your good work.

Nobody should specialize in one area to the total neglect of the others. Especially in junior faculty, versatility is extremely desirable. Every professor ought to be at least competent as both a teacher and a scholar. Teaching is a major part of what all academics do, and there is no excuse for doing it badly. An academic career lasts several decades; a teacher who does not keep up with the scholarship in the field will be obsolete long before retirement. Teaching and scholarship nourish and support each other, and many other kinds of activity help maintain a department, an institution, and a profession. Nobody can do everything, but the real leaders in the profession combine excellence in teaching and scholarship with the willingness to serve their colleagues and society.

- Update your dossier.
- Get new letters from new recommenders.
- Explain your job situation in your letter of application.
- Consult the department chair early about promotion criteria.
- Consult the department chair regularly about your own status.
- If you want to retain your job, be sensitive to the institution's priorities.
- Be sure you have usable evidence of your best work.
- Do not totally neglect any area of achievement valued by your institution.

3: COMMUNITY AND JUNIOR COLLEGES

Although many steps in the job-seeking and recruitment processes in community and junior colleges are similar to those in four-year institutions, there are enough variations to justify a few additional comments and recommendations to both candidates and departments.

ADVICE TO JOB CANDIDATES

The employment picture in community and junior colleges has recently begun to resemble that in BA-granting institutions. Though overall enrollments have risen, most of the increase has occurred in the vocational and technical fields that prepare students to enter the job market as soon as they complete their studies. In the humanities, however, this kind of growth has not taken place, and in consequence there appear to be even fewer full-time teaching positions now than there were a few years ago.

If you have given serious thought to teaching in a community or junior college but have never attended or taught in one, you should begin by learning all you can about this sector of postsecondary education. The list printed in the September issue of *PMLA* will give you an idea of the number and range of the colleges; further factual information can be obtained from the most current issue of the annual *Community and Junior College Directory*, published by the American Association of Community and Junior Colleges (1 Dupont Circle, NW, Washington, DC 20036), which not only lists the colleges by state but provides data on their affiliations, control, programs, enrollments, and number of faculty. From the large and growing bibliography of works on teaching in community and junior colleges, we recommend especially *Teaching in a Junior College* by Roger H. Garrison and *Guidelines for Junior College Teacher Training Programs*, issued by the Conference on College Composition and Communication. The former pamphlet discusses in detail the various types of colleges, the expectations they place on their faculty, and the special problems and rewards of teaching in these institutions. The CCCC guidelines cite, among other things, the attitudes and abilities needed for successful teaching in a community or junior college.

The instructional programs of community and junior colleges fall into three broad categories: transfer programs, vocational or technical studies, and continuing education. The proportions of the three categories will depend on the size, location, and constituency of the college. Some junior and community colleges are predominantly liberal arts institutions, at which most students are preparing to transfer to a BA-granting college after receiving the Associate in Arts degree from the two-year institution; as in California or Florida, the college may be part of a state system in which articulation with the colleges of the state university system works extremely well. Other community or junior colleges are primarily vocational and are set up to provide students with the skills required by business, industry, and certain professions; programs may range from nursing and physical therapy to data processing, law enforcement, and aviation technology. Continuing education programs typically serve students of all ages with a wide range of backgrounds, occupations, and interests. A small community or junior college may have elements of all three categories or may specialize in one; the larger colleges usually offer a comprehensive set of courses to serve the needs of all three groups of students.

The rich variety of programs and courses at community and junior colleges makes extensive generalization nearly impossible. If you are interested in teaching in one of these colleges, begin by looking carefully at the specific institutions to which you plan to apply. Examine the range of offerings in English, languages, and related subjects. Visit one or two nearby colleges, and try to arrange in advance to talk with faculty and students. The size, student body, and curriculum of the college will reflect the social and economic complexion of the community, and you will need to become familiar with these local conditions in order to judge whether you can offer something to the college and would be happy working with its students.

Because every community and junior college attempts to respond to the specific needs of its students, any given college may offer a considerable number of special programs, ranging from remedial to honors work, and a variety of instructional formats, including lectures, group discussions, and individualized assignments. The chief criteria for hiring new faculty at such a college are likely to be the teaching ability and attitude of the prospective teacher. Perhaps the most valuable asset a community or junior college teacher can have is flexibility—a willingness to attempt new techniques, to adapt to changing conditions, and, above all, to provide individualized instruction and counseling when necessary. For most faculty members, the philosophy of the community and junior college presupposes a belief that all students are educable and a predisposition toward encouraging student success in the classroom.

PREPARING TO APPLY FOR POSITIONS

As suggested above, learn as much as you can in advance about any college to which you plan to apply. If it is too far away to visit, be sure at least to read the catalog and study in detail the programs of the department or division to which you are applying. As you prepare to write, consider which of your academic credentials would be most appropriate to the position you seek. Consider also any special skills or abilities you have that may prove useful assets in a community or junior college situation. Measure your experience against the criteria and needs of the college to which you are applying. Ask yourself the following questions: (1) What are the stated aims or purposes of the college? How do your background and experience fit these aims? (2) Who are its students? Is your own experience in school and in life at all parallel to theirs? How would your experience be useful in the instruction of the type of students at this college? (3) How is the department or division organized? What are your specific qualifications to teach the courses it offers? The answers to these questions will help give you a clearer idea of the special nature of the institution and your possible relation to it. Whether you hold the PhD or not, it is important to review your education and experience carefully so that you can judge how you measure up to the special requirements of the junior or community college. You cannot always assume that having a PhD will give you an edge; you may be competing against MAs with a strong interdisciplinary background or with years of pertinent and valuable teaching experience. Attempt to ascertain in advance the specific hiring preferences, if any, of the colleges to which you are applying.

PREPARING THE VITA AND LETTER OF APPLICATION

Preparation of the vita and letter does not differ substantially from the procedures outlined in chapter 2, but many junior and community colleges have their own standardized application forms. Inquire first and, if there is such a form, request one in the mail. If possible, you should also secure advice from someone who has had experience in the kind of college to which you are applying. Both the letter and the résumé should be as detailed as possible, especially in the areas of particular concern to the community or junior college and its students.

INTERVIEWS

The interview is the time to obtain the information that correspondence and the catalog have not revealed. Having read the catalog, you have an idea of the structure and size of the department or division, and you may then wish to explore further the department's policies regarding your obligations. You may wish to ask about chances for advancement and the specific criteria that will be applied.

On the receiving end, you should be prepared to answer questions about your approaches to teaching regular or remedial courses. Needless to say, you should be honest in your replies. If a question draws a blank, answer directly with a forthright "I don't know." Bluffing is generally recognized by seasoned interviewers.

A final note. These suggestions will certainly not secure you a position, but they should make you aware that finding employment at the junior or community college level entails much more than producing numerous copies of your vita and mailing them to institutions selected at random. Many two-year institutions have clearly defined and distinctive characteristics, and all require special kinds of skill and commitment from teachers.

- Pay attention to the individual characteristics of junior and community colleges.
- Evaluate your qualifications in terms of the needs of the institutions you apply to.
- Emphasize your relevant qualifications in your vita, letters of application, and interviews.

4: THE NONACADEMIC JOB SEARCH

NEW CAREER PATTERNS FOR HUMANITIES PHDS

Because of the depressed academic job market during the seventies, a significant number of humanities PhDs moved quietly into a wide range of nonacademic careers in both the public and private sectors. Most of these enterprising pioneers found their own employment: they sought the advice and contacts of friends, families, and professors; they took civil service examinations; they answered classified advertisements. On the whole, they had no formal training beyond the PhD. By the end of the seventies, in addition to this unheralded search for employment outside the academy, highly publicized institutional efforts helped PhDs find jobs in the business world. Some PhDs enrolled in the well-advertised Careers in Business programs set up at various universities; others participated in more limited programs, such as Scholars in Transition, run by the Institute for Research in History; still others attended brief special conferences organized by universities and professional associations to instruct participants in "marketing" themselves as they were, without additional training, and to provide opportunities for PhDs to meet with business representatives. Initially, the media presented these PhDs as victims, sometimes of an unstable market, sometimes of a deliberately exploitative system. Frequently, they were portrayed as driving taxis and doing other kinds of work inappropriate for their educations.

We are now beginning to learn more about the PhDs who left the academy. In *Departing the Ivy Halls: Changing Employment Situations for Recent Ph.D.s*, Susan Henn and Betty D. Maxfield report that in 1981, 800 (14.3%) of those receiving PhDs in English and American language and literature from 1973 to 1976 held jobs in nonacademic settings; 600 (21.7%) of those receiving degrees in the other languages during this period held nonacademic jobs (58). (Nonacademic settings include elementary and secondary schools, business and industry, self-employment, government, hospitals and clinics, private foundations, other not-for-profit organizations, and other employers.) They conclude that "almost one-fourth of the individuals who had earned humanities doctorates within the last eight years were working in nonacademic job settings, compared to only 6 percent of the 1960-1964 Ph.D.'s" (61). When these PhDs were asked why they sought such employment, 44% of those in English studies reported they did so because academic jobs were not available; almost as large a group (37.3%) said that nonacademic work offered "a more attractive career option." Of those with degrees in other languages, 59.3% reported that academic positions in their fields were not available; 25.4% reported that more attractive career options were available (59). (Other reasons cited, but in small percentages, were pay, family constraints, and "other.")

The recognition of nonacademic employment as offering "a more attractive career option" is significant not only for PhDs but for those who contemplate entering a graduate degree program and for those who teach in such programs. This response and the information gathered from two additional studies of PhDs employed outside the academy indicate that the movement of PhDs into nonacademic employment involves something more than a temporary and desperate adjustment to oversupply. We now know that humanities PhDs can find satisfactory employment outside the academy. Lewis C. Solmon reports that humanities and nonhumanities PhDs holding a range of government jobs are in positions he judges appropriate for the highly trained. He also reports that most of them believe they are working at a professional level commensurate with their educa-tion. Ernest R. May and Dorothy G. Blaney, using Solmon's data and additional data drawn from studies of humanities PhDs working in the private sector, report higher levels of job satisfaction among PhDs outside the academy than among those within. They con-clude that "all people who are enthralled by literature, history, or philosophy are not neces-sarily people for whom teaching offers the most satisfying career" (75-76). These statistical studies are reinforced by positive reports from the PhDs employed outside the academy who have assisted in developing the Corporate Connections project, the business divi-sion of the MLA Job Information Service.

Perhaps the most important finding to those concerned with humanities programs is that a majority of humanities PhDs in nonacademic employment find their traditional graduate education useful (Solmon 99; May and Blaney 60). May and Blaney conclude, "although graduate training is an asset for people who become teachers, it is equally an asset for those who pursue other careers. . . . Teachers and nonteachers alike see it as having enhanced critical thinking and ability to do research, the latter something almost as prized outside academe as within it" (93-96). These studies suggest that our old assumption–that doctoral study serves only to train professors–has been unnecessarily narrow.

In the light of these findings, May and Blaney suggest that the following statement might be made to graduating college seniors:

> If you want to do graduate work in the humanities, your reason is probably interest in the subject rather than a well-considered inclination to pursue a career in college teaching.
>
> Graduate training will sharpen your critical faculties, give you some research skills, and perhaps equip you to do some scholarly writing. It could open up to you the possibility of a spell as a college teacher, conceivably even a lifetime in that occupa-tion, and you cannot otherwise add that option to your string.
>
> But you should not enroll in graduate school on the assumption that teaching in college is even what you *want* to do, let alone what you *will* do.
>
> If you end up in a line of work where an advanced degree in humanities is not a job qualification, the opportunity cost of your time in graduate school will obviously not have been zero. On the other hand, it will not necessarily turn out to have been high. Although your pay and status may at first be lower than if you had gone to work sooner, there is a good chance that in the long run you will do a better job and be better compensated by virtue of the finer tuning of your critical faculties and research talents.
>
> So think chiefly about whether you want graduate training for its own sake rather than for the sake of the job for which it might qualify you. Reckon the costs, includ-ing the possible opportunity costs, and make your decision accordingly. (96)

What does this mean for the new PhD who cannot find a full-time, tenure-track position and is eager to establish a career, for the untenured faculty member whose line has been eliminated, or for the tenured faculty member who each term grows less enchanted with teaching? Simply that other possibilities may be available–depending on your age; on your skills, background, personality, and interests; and on your ingenuity and perhaps your willingness to establish additional credentials. If from the start of your graduate school career you accepted that you might be one of the (roughly) four out of every ten English and foreign language PhDs to leave the academy, you will be in a better position– psychologically and practically–to control the next stage in your career. You should decide in advance the point at which you will turn from the academic job search or the unsatisfactory teaching job to another kind of career. There are two points to keep in mind as you prepare for this possibility. First, though the transition may take some time, finally you are likely to find a job. Laure M. Sharp notes that despite the weak academic job market, "periodic national surveys never confirmed the existence of high unemployment rates for humanists; (2.9% in 1977, 2.2% in 1979, and 1.5% in 1981)" (l). Second, timing is important. Age is not supposed to be a factor in hiring, but it often is, both within and outside the academy. Not only are PhDs who spend too many years in temporary or part-time teaching positions unlikely to be perceived as desirable candidates for tenure-track positions, they are also likely, when they do turn away from teaching, to find the job search outside the academy more difficult. For these reasons you should be hardheaded about limiting the number of years you spend in marginal teaching positions. You may be better off taking your future in your own hands and leaving the academy before you suffer the discouragement of a negative tenure decision or the burnout that often accompanies holding too many part-time and temporary positions.

If you still have the option of an academic job, how can you find out whether you should be thinking about a business career? If you have no option, how do you start the transition process? One way is to locate and talk to PhDs who have made the transition; another is to read about the process in such books as Richard N. Bolles's *What Color Is Your Parachute?* or Richard Irish's *Go Hire Yourself an Employer.* Yet another—a more expensive way—is to enroll in one of the special programs developed by business schools for humanities PhDs. Somewhere in between fall the MLA's workshops, which are run by a specialist in executive recruiting and held in conjunction with the MLA convention. They are modestly priced, and they survey the problem of moving from the academy to the business world, describe some kinds of jobs available in business, and discuss the job-search process. Participants also meet individually with the workshop leader to talk about developing their résumés. Whenever possible, workshop participants are given introductions to PhDs with established careers outside the academy who are willing to give advice about the job search in particular industries.

THE PSYCHOLOGY OF BEGINNING

Although certain kinds of work in publishing, corporate communications, technical writing, and translating have traditionally attracted PhDs seeking nonacademic positions, virtually every type of business—from insurance and banking to manufacturing and heavy industry—needs educated, trained personnel with the ability to do research, to organize thoughts and ideas into clear and concise prose, and to deal effectively with associates. Good opportunities in business do exist, but you will have to seek them out. Searching for a nonacademic position is every bit as demanding and emotionally draining as the search for a teaching job, but if you are properly prepared, the search can be stimulating and challenging. Reports from those who have made the transition indicate that you can learn a good deal about yourself in the process. You may even discover abilities you did not know you possessed.

If from the start of your graduate education you face the possibility of multiple career options, you will probably find the prospect of a transition less difficult than will those who ignore the possibility. You must first accept that you can do little to increase your chances of landing a good academic job in a depressed market. Every candidate who has looked for a teaching job since the early seventies has been in competition with hundreds of other applicants at every college to which he or she applied. When a department has that many applicants to choose from, chance certainly plays a role in the screening procedures; no one would suggest that a department can unerringly choose the one "best" candidate among five hundred or more applicants. Once you realize that there is nothing wrong with you or with your background, you can begin to gear yourself for the job hunt. You must make up your mind to leave college teaching and turn all your efforts toward finding a nonacademic job. (You need not, of course, leave your work as a scholar.) Many business executives believe that former academics will rush back to the academy at the first offer of a teaching position, and they are likely to recognize a halfhearted effort. In order to convince them of your sincerity, you must be committed to finding a job in business.

Also, you must realize that no one outside academe will hire you simply because you have a PhD. Your degree can be a selling point, but you must find a way to convince prospective employers that it is a symbol of what you can do in the future, not a reward for what you have done in the past. You do not have to hide your education, but you must have more to offer than your academic credentials. You should not assume that your move out of the academy will mean a move from an intellectual to a nonintellectual environment. Intellectuals are not found exclusively in colleges and universities; many people outside academe have strong intellectual interests, and many are active researchers and writers. The challenge of the right kind of job for you can be no less—and perhaps even more—rewarding than teaching. Perhaps the best way to describe the psychological reorientation that a job candidate must undergo is to quote the suggestions of a PhD in English who is now a happy and successful insurance salesman.

You have to realize that no one is going to hand you a job like they do in the academic world, where you write a letter, wait for an interview, and then wait for a faceless committee to select you. You have to . . . go out there and find one, even create one if need be. The first problem is how. Being a student of any kind is demoralizing since you are always being told you are wrong; and being a humanities graduate student is worse, since even tenured faculty are walking lightly these days. When job-hunting, see your friends at home and stay the hell out of the English department. The first thing I would do (*did*) would be to go to the bookstore and buy Irish or one of those success books that academics look down upon, and read the goddam thing. . . . Remember, if you survived four years of grad school, if you taught freshmen and still passed your exams, and especially if you earned your Ph.D., you are a success right now. Very few people have the endurance, ambition, and mental agility to do what you have done. My Ph.D. was one of my main selling points. . . . The insurance people [saw] this right off; they knew instinctively why I went through graduate school and I was surprised when they told me that they thought highly of my degree. So number one: get some self-confidence; shake off the cynical pomposity of academia and feel good about yourself. You have already done more than most people ever do and you have the power to do more than you ever dreamed you could.

WHAT DO YOU WANT TO DO?

The first question you must ask yourself is "If I can't teach, what do I want to do?" How specifically you answer that question will have more to do with your future job satisfaction than any other part of the job search will. Don't give in to despair and take the first job that comes along.

There are many ways to discover jobs that interest you. The first and most obvious way is simply to ask yourself what you would like to do. Do not rule out anything that you like until you are absolutely certain that you cannot do it or that you cannot make a living doing it. If you are not certain what you want to do or if you simply want to explore all your options, there are several ways to get help: (1) Almost every college or university has a counseling center with career counselors who will help you at no charge. (2) Talk with as many friends who are employed outside academe as you can. (3) Consult the *Occupational Outlook Handbook*, published biennially by the Bureau of Labor Statistics, U. S. Department of Labor (Washington: GPO).

In order to decide what kind of job you want you must make a careful assessment of your skills, needs, work patterns, strengths, and weaknesses. You must decide exactly what working conditions are important to you: Are you willing to travel? Do you want to work nine to five, or do you prefer a more flexible schedule? Do you prefer to work alone or as part of a group? Is the industry, the location, or the type of job most important?

Next, you should try to find out the duties associated with different job categories, the special abilities or training needed, the kinds of companies that offer jobs of that sort, the opportunities for advancement in these occupations, and the salary range. Most of this information can be picked up from people already in the field; it's a good idea to talk with several individuals in jobs that interest you. They not only can provide valuable information about their jobs but can often refer you to acquaintances in similar or related jobs. You will have begun to develop a chain of contacts. Above all, do not be afraid to ask people about their work. Usually they will be flattered, no matter how "important" they are, and most will be candid about what they like and dislike in their jobs.

SHOULD YOU RETRAIN?

At some point before you begin searching for a job, you must decide whether or not to retrain. Usually retraining is not necessary. Two recent surveys found that of the PhDs who went into business, 95% found their first business job without any further training. For some jobs, of course, retraining is essential: if you decide to become a lawyer, as numerous PhDs in language and literature have done lately, you must go to law school. There are several ways to go about retraining without going into debt: If you have not yet completed your PhD, you might ask your department for permission to minor in a subject not traditionally associated with English or foreign-languages (e.g., library science, journalism, or business administration). If you have completed or nearly completed your graduate program or if you have been bypassed by a tenure vote, you might ask to be retained as a part-time instructor for a year or two while you take courses in a new subject. If all else fails, explore the possibility of fellowships, scholarships, or even assistantships in other departments. If you have decided that you must retrain, do not be timid. Go to your department—that is, to a meeting of the senior professors, not just the department head—present your problem, and ask for a part-time or teaching-assistant appointment while you retrain.

WHEN TO START AND HOW LONG TO LOOK

Once you have a good idea about what you want to do, you should plan on spending an extended period—often six months to a year—looking for a job; the higher the job you seek, the longer it will take. Do not start looking for a job in business, however, until you are ready to accept one. Unlike universities, some of which begin recruiting as much as a year in advance of the starting date, corporations normally recruit and hire for immediate openings and therefore expect new employees to begin working within two weeks or a month.

One of the most difficult problems that you will face during your search is likely to be financial. If you are in debt for your education, go to your creditors, explain your situation, and assure them that as soon as you are employed you will pay your debts. Meanwhile, finance your search as cheaply and efficiently as you can. Penury is nothing new to most graduate students, and you must believe that a few more months of privation will ultimately pay off. If part-time employment is necessary, begin by trying to convince your department to carry you as a part-time instructor while you look for a job. Teaching part-time, you will have a flexible schedule that will allow you to work hard at interviewing. Make it clear to the department head that the appointment is for only one semester or one academic year and that it is only a temporary measure to ward off starvation. Your primary occupation is job seeking, and the more time you have to work toward employment, the quicker you will be employed.

ASSEMBLING YOUR CREDENTIALS

In academic circles, the standard procedure for introducing oneself to a prospective employer is through a letter accompanying a curriculum vitae. For a business job, you should use a cover letter and a good business résumé.

1. The cover letter. (See sample letter in appendix C.) Each cover letter must be prepared carefully and individually. You must anticipate and overcome the incredulity of the reader, who will at first almost surely be surprised and even a little skeptical about an application from a PhD in language or literature. Since you cannot speak to the reader personally, you must use all your rhetorical skills to project an image that will seem ideal for the position. In particular, there are three techniques that seem to have good results. First, if you are answering an ad, repeat a good deal of the language of the ad itself; this suggests familiarity with the responsibilities of the position. Second, learn and use the language of the business community. Third, do not be modest.

2. The résumé. (See sample in appendix C.) You must prepare a good business résumé, not an academic vita. Do not include the title of your dissertation or a detailed description of all the courses you have taken or taught. Résumés should be succinct, distinctive, and easy to read; they should use active verbs and straightforward constructions. Do not use any negatives. Everything should present the most positive picture. Stress the managerial side of academic training: your ability to teach basic writing skills, your ability to do independent research, your administrative or editorial experience, and your ability to organize and analyze. Familiarize yourself with business terminology, and then translate your own training and experience into it. The translation is not so difficult as you may think: designing and implementing new courses qualify as "administrative experience," as does committee work; in interviewing and counseling students you have done "personnel work." Publications, however scholarly, demonstrate your ability to do research, to assimilate information, and, of course, to write. Undergraduate courses in economics, or business, or even in organizational psychology probably merit more attention than do graduate seminars in Elizabethan drama or Victorian poetry. Stress all your practical accomplishments—positions of leadership, extracurricular activities, volunteer community and social work, and so forth. Finally, your résumé must be printed on good-quality paper, and it must be short (preferably one page, never more than two). Also, it must be aimed directly at your prospective employer.

3. Recommendations. It is imperative that you have your academic letters of reference redone to reflect a more general background. Go to your advisers, explain your situation, and have them rewrite the academic recommendations, playing down your "brilliant work on Restoration comedy" and praising instead your ways with the world: managerial skills, writing and speaking skills, persuasiveness, self-confidence, dynamic personality, and ability to work independently. Make sure that your advisers know how to write such recommendations. If necessary, make polite but forceful suggestions. If someone in the business community knows you—someone for whom you worked one summer or who has known you for a long time—by all means ask for a recommendation. It may be worth more than a letter from the leading scholar in your field.

WHERE TO LOOK

Ignore no opening that interests you and for which you are even remotely qualified. Start by using the total resources of your institution. It is important that you make yourself known to the director of your university placement service and to those individuals responsible for placing students and alumni in positions in business and industry. The best way to do this is simply to speak frankly with the placement officer about what you think you might like to do. Ask for advice about the kinds of positions for which you might be suited and for suggestions about local business opportunities. Let the placement officer know that you are eager to interview for positions, and give him or her your business résumé to circulate when the opportunity arises. If you receive no specific leads, ask for the names of people in the local community whom you might consult. Find out from the placement officer which corporations hold interviews on your campus, and then take advantage of as many interviews as possible. Although corporations normally direct their campus interviews toward candidates for the BA, you will find that most representatives are willing to speak to graduate students and experienced teachers as well. Even if the interviews do not lead to a definite offer, they will teach you a great deal about the kinds of opportunities that are available.

After you have used your placement service to develop your interview skills and to create a chain of contacts, begin going through the classified section of the major newspapers in your area each day, and either write or telephone for an interview when you see an interesting ad. Do not undersell yourself—either in terms of salary requirements or your ability to do the job—but keep in mind that, since you are trying to enter an entirely new field, you cannot expect to start at the top. Once a company becomes interested in you, there is usually room to negotiate about the starting salary and benefits. You might also consider taking a good entry-level position. Remember that the skills and experience you gain in your first job will not only make you a likely candidate for promotion but should also make you more attractive to other corporations.

Personal contacts can be very helpful. Begin by visiting the business school on your campus. If you do not know a member of the faculty, someone in your department should be able to give you an introduction, or you can simply introduce yourself. Ask for advice about local firms and for the name of anyone who might be able to give you information.

If possible, get the person who gives you the name to call the contact and give you a brief introduction. Follow up with a call of your own, saying that you are seriously interested in finding a job in business and asking whether the contact would be willing to speak with you about general opportunities. Business people are normally more than willing to talk to academics. Keep these interviews on an informal "I am seeking information and advice" basis, but do not hesitate, if things go well, to ask the names of others with whom you might be able to talk. If the person is impressed and thinks you might fit into the firm, you may be referred to a colleague who could be of direct help. If you do receive additional leads, ask whether you can use your contact's name, and, if so, be sure to mention it. It is always easier to arrange an interview if you know someone.

If you have family contacts or influential neighbors and friends, by all means ask them for help. If not, go to your professors and ask whether they have friends or neighbors working in business who might be willing to speak with you. If you want to leave academe, you must deal with people of some stature in different fields, and you begin by meeting them. Once you meet one person, get the names of others and follow up, thus building chains of contacts. Do not be timid.

Among the more interesting ways to find a job is to pick out an organization that interests you and simply create a job for yourself. This approach may sound preposterous, but it is not. The trick is to choose an organization that you can research thoroughly. Your research should include several steps: (1) Talk to as many people who are employed in the organization as you can—from secretaries to the president. (2) Try to isolate all the problems that you can help solve. (3) Read up on the general problems and goals of similar organizations. (4) Write a proposal explaining how you could help the organization to function more effectively—in other words, write a well-researched seminar paper using the language of the business. (5) Finally, arrange an interview with the highest official who will see you, making sure that you are talking to someone with the authority to hire you. Once you have gained an interview, it is essential that you keep it low-key. Under no circumstances should your interviewer get the impression that you want him or her to offer you a job immediately. After you have made your proposal, simply explain that you are available if the firm should wish to get in touch with you. Follow up the interview by periodically reminding your interviewer of your proposal. Here again, you must be gentle but confident and forceful. As incredible as it may sound, several language and literature PhDs have found jobs this way.

THE INTERVIEW

Without a doubt the interview is the most important part of your job search. Whenever possible, arrange to talk first with the official who has the authority to hire you. How you reach him or her depends on the structure of the organization and on your own persistence and ingenuity.

At the beginning of your job search, try to schedule several "practice" interviews in order to gain interviewing experience and to learn how to relax, present yourself attractively, and translate your academic experience into forms that nonacademic employers appreciate. It is important to gain wide interviewing experience so that you will be comfortable and confident when you begin to interview for jobs that you really want. During the practice interviews, you should learn to answer the three questions most often asked of PhDs: Why are you leaving the academy for business? Why are you interested in working for us? What kind of person are you anyway? Once you have gone through an interview training period, you can begin to schedule interviews for jobs that attract you. Allow time for research and thinking before the interview. Talk with someone already employed in the organization in order to get a preliminary impression of what to expect. Be prepared to talk the language of the employer without being insincere or condescending. Moreover, it is essential to plan a few things to say in case conversation lags. Seeing the inside of the building the day before will make everything associated with the interview seem less strange. By this time you should be well informed about the firm's personnel needs, about what it does for its clients, and about how you can be useful to the firm. For example, a PhD in English who is now employed on the editorial board of a nationally circulated magazine spent three days studying back issues of the publication before she went for the interview. When she did go, she knew the magazine's format thoroughly and could refer to its standard features easily. She was prepared to give short critiques of the stylistic elements of the magazine, but she was careful to demonstrate the full range of her editorial ability by critiquing in detail the language of a rival publication. Such preparation is time-consuming, but it usually produces results.

Since PhDs are still an oddity to the open job market, remember that your extensive education may occasionally intimidate an employer. Be friendly, pleasant, and relaxed, and do not use the title of "doctor" unless it is appropriate for the position you seek. At the same time, never apologize for your years in graduate school.

THE FOLLOW-UP

Following each informal chat or formal interview, send a brief note thanking the person for his or her time and help and expressing interest in the firm. Don't hesitate to phone back for additional information. Such calls indicate interest. You can also use the follow-up note to underline things you said or to point out aspects of the firm that you like. Do not be bashful; follow up several times if necessary. If you have heard nothing after a week or two, phone or write, adding some new information about yourself and expressing a continuing interest in the firm.

ADVICE FROM A PHD WHO IS NOW IN BUSINESS

It's impossible to describe the emotional impact, both "highs" and "lows," of a radical career switch—from language professor to engineer. So, instead, I've decided to address three questions I've often been asked by fellow PhDs considering changing careers.

1. What do you do now and do you like it?
Three years ago, after eight years of teaching German, French, and English, and a PhD in German linguistics, I decided to leave the academy. I took a position with Hewlett-Packard as a marketing engineer in a "customer training" department. But believe me, I didn't know what I was getting into! The original job description said I would design training materials to be used in teaching customers how to use new HP computer software products. That sounded straightforward. At that time I would have never believed I was about to become a computer buff. After all, I was really a humanist at heart, wasn't I?

My self-training program started with learning to use a word processor. Then I advanced to using a text editor and computer graphics. Before I knew it I was learning about files and data bases and inquiry languages. I had moved into the world of data management. Soon I started wondering about the architecture of the Hewlett-Packard 3000 computer and how it manipulates data. Ye gads, I was talking in bits and bytes! Next, the concept of computers communicating with other computers began to fascinate me, so I entered the field of data communications. Now I worry about how cryptic information is transmitted across telephone lines and satellites through services called public data networks. What next?

I suppose this means I'm hooked. Of what value have I been to HP? Well, I've designed, written, tested, and evaluated several training programs for new software products. I've tested and assisted in the development of new products. I've taught classes, given demos, developed training procedures, trained trainers and course developers, coordinated training projects. I've worked on training issues across divisions of HP in the United States and Europe. I've given formal and informal presentations, both in the United States and in Europe. As you can imagine, my foreign language skills come in handy for some of these tasks.

This synopsis of my engineering career answers half of my original question. I hope that you have also grasped that I am very happy in my new career and have no regrets about leaving the academy. There are indeed certain elements of the teaching profession that I miss—the university environment, contact with students, research resources, flexible work schedules. But, in my case, the positives outweigh the negatives. Being able to choose where I want to live and work, job security, a healthy income, as well as an exciting and challenging career certainly tell me that I made the right move.

2. What advice do you have for people with backgrounds similar to yours interested in making a similar career switch?

It took me sixteen months of researching and soul-searching to make the decision to leave teaching, to decide what I wanted to do, and to get the job. Here are my hints to you:

a. Do your homework! You've got a lot of research experience, and career changing is your most important research project. Don't treat it lightly! Use some of the better-known books on the market (such as Richard Bolles's *What Color Is Your Parachute?* or Richard Lathrop's *Who's Hiring Who?*) and talk to at least fifty people who do not work with you now about their jobs, their fields, their companies.

b. First decide what industry interests you, then the particular companies. Go to visit the companies—anybody you know there can get you in the front door. (If you can't find anybody who works there, bump into somebody in the parking lot!) Don't be timid. You want to get in the front door, so that you can proceed with your research, not to apply for a job (at first). Do this with at least four or five companies; talk to people in four or five different departments in each. Some departments to try would be technical publications, technical training, marketing, product marketing, sales development, sales training, marketing communications, support. Remember, one person gets you in the door; that person knows other people, who know other people. . . . Make as many contacts as you can.

c. Don't send out a zillion résumés or apply for jobs in the paper. But do keep in touch with your "personal contacts"—especially in the company you've decided to work for. They will know what jobs are available. When you find the type of job you want and who runs that department, call or visit him or her, just for more information about what the department does. By this time, you know the right people, the buzzwords, and the job descriptions. Write your resumé around what you've learned and any related experience you have, not around all your experience. You are ready to express your interest in a position.

d. Now timing is key. You must make your interest and qualifications known to the right people . . . and be persistent. Frequent (about once a week), short (3- or 4-minute) phone calls work best. If you've narrowed it down to the type of job you want and three or four people who could hire you in each of two or three companies, you'll be making a lot of short phone calls. Send your résumé to those people and follow up consistently. When there's an opening, you want them to think of you—it saves them the trouble of going to personnel.

Be choosy; do not take the first thing that comes along. If you've done your home-work, you'll get several offers—then the choice is yours.

Remember, active participation in the job search is necessary—make contacts, visit companies, meet people, get referrals, make phone calls; blindly sending out letters and résumés or answering ads usually doesn't work.

3. What are some job titles in industry that might be suitable for people with writing, teaching, and research skills?

Most books on the market tell you to analyze your skills and interests and then match them with jobs in industry. But the step of finding job titles is difficult. The professional employment part of the classified ads of a large newspaper can be helpful, but here are a few job titles to research:

marketing associate	reliability engineer
support engineer	scientific writer
marketing researcher	sales representative
technical support engineer	editor
marketing engineer	sales center engineer
on-line support engineer	technical editor
training specialist	sales development engineer
off-line support engineer	grant and proposal writer
instructional technologist	office products coordinator
quality assurance engineer	product marketing manager
technical writer	personnel administrator

Make sure you realize that you do not have to go back to school and complete a new degree to make a career switch, even to a technical field. Most companies are willing to train the right people. But you must be able to show some related experience or training to get the job initially. Often, current enrollment in a related class will do the trick; a couple of courses completed in the field is better.

Leverage off your experience. In completing your PhD you acquired many different skills—research, writing, teaching, organizational skills, negotiating, presentation, and, possibly, statistical analysis, word processing, computer programming. And you un-doubtedly excel in communication skills. If you know enough about the job and believe that you can do it, then you can convince someone to hire you for it. Be confident and assertive. If you've accomplished a PhD, you can handle any job you're given.

Donna M. Senko
Marketing Engineer
Information Networks Division
Hewlett-Packard

- Be aware that many literature and language PhDs have successful careers outside the academy.
- Keep your morale high.
- Commit yourself fully to whatever career you choose.
- Assess your PhD training and academic experience in terms of the requirements of your nonacademic career possibilities.
- Investigate job opportunities related to your interests.
- Consider retraining, but do not assume that retraining is necessary in all fields.
- Plan to spend six months to a year looking for a job.
- Prepare your credentials so as to make a favorable impression on nonacademic employers, in both content and format.
- Explore all possible leads to job opportunities: placement offices, newspaper classified ads, personal contacts, research on employers.
- Prepare for interviews and follow them up.
- Read about career options and job hunting.
- Be positive, imaginative, persistent.

WHAT TO READ

I. Career Options for the Humanities PhD

Bestor, Dorothy K. *Aside from Teaching, What in the World Can You Do?* Seattle: U of Washington P, 1982 (available through the MLA).

Brod, Richard I., Elizabeth Cowan, and Neal Woodruff, eds. *English and Foreign Languages: Employment and the Profession.* Special joint issue of the ADE and ADFL *Bulletins.* New York: MLA, 1976.

Fox, Marcia R. *Put Your Degree to Work: A Career-Planning and Job-Hunting Guide for the New Professional.* New York: Norton, 1979 (available through the MLA).

Harwood, John T. "From Genre Theory to the Want Ads." *ADE Bulletin* 44 (1975): 21-24.

———. "Nonacademic Job Hunting." *AAUP Bulletin* Sept. 1974: 313-16.

Jacobs, Rita D. *The Useful Humanists: Alternative Careers for PhDs in the Humanities.* New York: Rockefeller Foundation, 1977.

Jennings, Lane. "Unmaking Our Own Job Crises." *ADFL Bulletin* 6.4 (1975): 12-15.

Lehrer, Linda J. "Notes from the Outside." *ADE Bulletin* 54 (1977): 37-41.

Reilly, Kevin P., and Sheila A. Murdick, eds. *Teaching and Beyond: Nonacademic Career Programs for PhDs.* Albany: University of the State of New York, 1984.

Solmon, Lewis C., Nancy L. Ochsner, and Margo-Lea Hurwicz. *Alternative Careers for Humanities PhDs: Perspectives of Students and Graduates.* New York: Holt, 1980.

Sullivan, Edward D. "Alternative Careers." *ADFL Bulletin* 9.1 (1977): 27-29.

Wyman, Roger E., Nancy A. Risser, et al. *Humanities PhDs and Nonacademic Careers: A Guide for Faculty Advisers.* Evanston: Committee on Institutional Cooperation, 1983.

II. From the BA to the Marketplace

The following are written more for undergraduate than for graduate students, but they are enlightening and useful.

Beck, Robert E. *The Liberal Arts Major in Bell System Management.* Washington: Assn. of American Colleges, 1981.

Fuller, Carol S. "Language-Oriented Careers in the Federal Government." *ADFL Bulletin* 6.1 (1974): 45-51.

Gould, Christine A. *Consider Your Options: Business Opportunities for Liberal Arts Graduates.* Washington: Assn. of American Colleges, 1983.

Honig, Lucille J., and Richard I. Brod. *Foreign Languages and Careers.* New York: MLA, 1979.

Orange, Linwood E. *English: The Pre-Professional Major.* New York: MLA, 1979.

Shinkman, Christopher J. *Public and Non-Profit Sector Employment for Liberal Arts Graduates.* Washington: Assn. of American Colleges, 1982.

Warren, Russell G. *New Links between General Education and Business Careers.* Washington: Assn. of American Colleges, 1983.

Weinstein, Allen I. "Foreign Language Majors: The Washington Perspective." *ADFL Bulletin* 6.4 (1974): 18-27.

III. Practical Guides for the Nonacademic Job Seeker

Bolles, Richard Nelson. *What Color Is Your Parachute? A Practical Manual for Job-Hunters & Career Changers.* Berkeley: Ten Speed, 1984.

Bostwick, Burdette E. *One Hundred Eleven Proven Techniques and Interview Strategies for Getting the Job Interview.* New York: Wiley, 1981.

——— . *Résumé Writing: A Comprehensive How-to-Do-It Guide.* 2nd ed. New York: Wiley, 1980.

Irish, Richard K. *Go Hire Yourself an Employer.* Rev. ed. Garden City: Anchor-Doubleday, 1978.

Kotter, John P., et al. *Self-Assessment and Career Development.* Englewood Cliffs: Prentice, 1978.

Munschauer, John L. *Jobs for English Majors and Other Smart People.* Princeton: Peterson's Guides, 1981.

Uris, Auren. *The Executive Deskbook.* New York: Van Nostrand, 1976.

Welch, Mary Scott. *Networking.* New York: Harcourt, 1980.

For an expanded list of titles pertaining to career opportunities in specific nonacademic areas, you may wish to consult the following:

Donaldson, Christine F., and Elizabeth A. Flynn. *Alternative Careers for PhDs in the Humanities: A Selected Bibliography.* New York: MLA, 1982.

GOVERNMENT JOBS

(Most of the information in this section on federal government employment was taken from a pamphlet entitled *First, See Us,* published by the U. S. Office of Personnel Management.)

Finding a job with the federal government is somewhat different from finding a job in business or industry. To begin with, government employers are not nearly as skeptical or incredulous when a liberal arts PhD applies for a job as private employers are likely to be. Obtaining government work is a slow process, however; if you are lucky, you might be hired in four months, but you should plan on a search lasting from six to nine months.

Your chances for being hired depend on your qualifications, how fast vacancies are occurring in the region in which you want to work, the number of qualified applicants who want the same kind of job, and the salary level you say you will accept. Because the government's hiring needs vary over time and from one location to another, you might be able to apply in one location for a particular kind of job and be unable to apply for the same kind of work in another location. The most important thing is to be on the spot and to be persistent.

There is no list of all available government jobs. A list of the jobs available in your region, however, can be obtained at the nearest Federal Job Information Center. The Office of Personnel Management maintains the Federal Job Information Centers in several major metropolitan areas across the country. They are listed under "U. S. Government" in metropolitan-area phone directories. In addition, federal employment opportunities are posted in state job service (state employment security) offices. You might also check the government-documents section of your library or ask your university placement service for a list of government openings.

If you wish to apply for a government job, inquire at a Federal Job Information Center whether applications are being accepted in your area for the kind of work you want. Job information specialists may be able to suggest a type of job for which your education and experience qualify you. Government jobs are classified by grade levels based on level of difficulty and responsibility. Salaries correspond to the grades; the higher the grade level, the higher the salary, regardless of the employee's qualifications. PhDs are usually found in jobs with a rating of GS-9 or above. A current listing of the pay scale for each grade level can be obtained at the Federal Job Information Center. If the government consistently needs applications for the kind of work you want, you will be asked to submit a complete application. Applications are not accepted when openings are not expected.

After you have filed your application and taken any necessary written tests, your name will go on the Office of Personnel Management list. When an opening occurs, your qualifications will be reviewed in relation to the requirements of the job. If you are among the best qualified, your name will be referred to the agency along with the names of the other best-qualified applicants. By law, agency hiring officials may choose from among the top three applicants referred to them for a particular job. The names of the applicants not selected are returned to the Office of Personnel Management for consideration for future vacancies.

Former VISTA, ACTION Community, and Peace Corps volunteers and leaders are given special opportunities in seeking Federal employment for one year after completion of service. (Under some circumstances, the period may be extended for two more years.) If you qualify, you do not have to compete with the applicant pool in order to be hired. An agency may hire you by simply establishing that you meet the minimum qualifications for a job. For further information, call a Federal Job Information Center.

In addition, some agencies are excepted from the competitive service procedures of the Office of Personnel Management. These agencies, which are listed below, have separate systems for hiring personnel, and job seekers should apply to them direct.

Personnel Office
U. S. Information Agency
301 4th St., SW
Washington, DC 20547

Director, Recruitment and Placement
Service
Veterans Administration
941 N. Capitol St., NE
Washington, DC 20421

Foreign Service Recruitment Division Office of Personnel
U. S. Department of State Federal Bureau of Investigation
P. O. Box 9317 Constitution Ave.
Rosslyn Station Washington, DC
Arlington, VA 22209 (apply to your local agency if
 possible)

Three useful publications for finding out about federal employment:

Federal Employees' Almanac (annual). Available for about $5 a copy from Federal Employees' Almanac, P. O. Box 457, Merrifield, VA 22116. About 150 pages of pay schedules, health insurance and other benefits, policies on various kinds of leave, training programs, the retirement system, veterans' preference, performance-appraisal systems, appeals and grievance systems, taxes, and legislation that allows or prohibits various activities for federal employees.

The United States Government Manual (annual). Available for about $10 a copy from Superintendent of Documents, U. S. Government Printing Office, Washington, DC 20402. About nine hundred pages describing the activities of all federal agencies, legislative, executive, and judicial, including independent agencies, government corporations, and commissions. The data for each agency include the names and titles of all current major officers (including personnel officers), the addresses and phone numbers of the agencies, directory information on the location and officers of all regional offices, and a breakdown of the work of each agency's principal divisions and most important programs.

Federal Career Opportunities (biweekly). Available for $6.50 a copy ($34 for 6 issues, $66 for 12, and $138 for 26) from Federal Research Service, Inc., Subscription Manager, 370 Maple Ave. W., Box 1059, Vienna, VA 22180. About 64 pages of very fine print listing all jobs open in the period of the issue, their closing dates, their identifying numbers, their location, and whom to make contact with for more information.

Libraries that are federal repositories (some university libraries are) may have copies of these publications.

A number of federal employers have tape-recorded "job banks" that are updated periodically (usually weekly). They list all openings in the period and explain the application procedure. Call the personnel offices of the agencies you are interested in and ask for the number.

Most federal agencies are administratively attached to the Office of Personnel Management, 1900 E St., NW, Washington, DC 20415. To ask for forms and find out what you must do to get on their qualified list with a government rating, call (202) 737-9616. The OPM has a library that is open to the public and that specializes (naturally) in information about employment. The librarians are very helpful and will provide photocopies of classification standards for various jobs (these standards are useful in wording the "narratives" on your application form, the SF 171).

WORKS CITED

Henn, Susan, and Betty D. Maxfield. *Departing the Ivy Halls: Changing Employment Situations for Recent Ph.D.s.* Washington: National Academy, 1983.

May, Ernest R., and Dorothy G. Blaney. *Careers for Humanists.* New York: Academic, 1981.

Sharp, Laure M. "The Employment Situation of Humanists: 1979-1981." Unpublished document, Bureau of Social Science Research, Inc., 1990 M Street, NW, Washington, DC 20036, 1984.

Solmon, Lewis C. *Underemployed Ph.D.'s.* Lexington: Heath, 1981.

5: ADVICE TO DEPARTMENTS

Department chairs and other senior members of the faculty play two important roles in every candidate's job search: hiring and placement. Hiring concerns all departments at one time or another; placement concerns primarily graduate departments, but every department should assume some responsibility for finding jobs for junior colleagues who do not receive tenure.

One of the most regrettable by-products of the difficult job market of the past several years has been the sense of alienation that many job seekers feel toward the profession, which, as they see it, has let them down badly. Some grievances have been directed toward specific individuals (such as department chairs) and have often been justified by instances of genuine mistreatment. The MLA alone has received enough complaints to demonstrate that the sense of frustration is serious and pervasive.

At the same time, anyone who has served as an academic administrator must sympathize with those chairs who, because of a lack of time or staff or because of pressures from higher administrative echelons, have been unable to make recruiting as personal and cordial as they would like. This chapter offers some guidelines for those who are already secure in the profession, especially those who are in some way involved in the recruitment or placement process.

In general, all senior faculty should stay aware of the conditions in the job market. Conditions have changed drastically over the past twenty years, and many of the customary procedures and normal expectations have changed at the same time. It would be useful for everyone to read manuals such as this one, not only the chapters intended for chairs and search committees but the sections addressed to the candidates as well. An ability to understand the situation from the perspective of the person on the other side of the negotiation is surely the crucial factor in restoring a measure of human sensitivity to an inevitably stressful process.

MLA POLICY STATEMENTS ON RECRUITING AND HIRING

Responsible members of the profession have long recognized that open and fair hiring practices and procedures are essential to the health of the profession. Resolutions passed by the MLA Executive Council and by the Executive Committees of the ADE and the ADFL have emphasized the moral as well as professional obligation of departments to list all vacancies openly, and federal regulations governing equal employment opportunity now make the open listing of positions a legal responsibility as well. In 1971, recognizing that departments did not always know whether vacancies would arise, the MLA created the *Job Information Lists* to give departments the opportunity to convey all kinds of information about hiring prospects, in addition to listing vacancies. Valuable as the *Lists* are to job candidates, the opportunity to publish statements every eight or ten weeks is of equal value to departments: when no hiring is possible, the department can reduce or eliminate unnecessary correspondence; if hiring is possible, it can attract applications from qualified and interested candidates—and only from such candidates. More than eighty percent of all four-year departments now participate regularly in the service.

Statement on Hiring

The MLA, especially through the Committee on Careers, the ADE, and the ADFL, regularly discusses policies and practices relating to the recruitment and hiring of faculty, and when appropriate it adopts a formal statement of policy. The following statement was adopted in 1977 and remains in force:

The MLA Advisory Committee on the Job Market [since renamed the Committee on Careers], the Association of Departments of English, and the Association of Departments of Foreign Languages affirm the necessity of adhering to fair and open hiring policies, practices, and procedures as an essential part of our moral, professional, and legal obligations. We urge that departments observe the suggestions given in the MLA's *Guide for Job Candidates and Department Chairmen in English and Foreign Languages.* And we urge compliance with the following guidelines when hiring new faculty members.

Guidelines for Hiring

1. Departments shall make regular use of the *Job Information Lists* to keep job seekers and professional organizations in the discipline informed about possibilities for employment and the current state of the job market.

2. Throughout any search for new faculty members the principles and guidelines of equal opportunity/affirmative action shall be adhered to.

3. Advertisements of openings shall be as specific as possible about the following: whether the opening is a definite, likely, or possible one; what possibility there is for tenure; minimal degree requirements; field(s) of expertise; minimal teaching experience; any other essential criteria.

4. Applicants shall be allowed ample time to respond to advertisements of openings, and whenever possible deadlines for application should be specified; normally applications should be accepted for at least 21 days after the publication of a given issue of the *Job Information Lists.*

5. Unless otherwise stated in the advertisement itself, applications in response to announcements should be acknowledged promptly and courteously in writing (if possible, within two weeks), and care should be taken to inform applicants of their status following the initial screening. [A later policy statement, which appears directly after these guidelines, also deals with the question of acknowledging applications.]

6. Candidates whose dossiers have been requested should be notified as soon as the departmental decision about their candidacy has been made.

7. No matter where interviews are conducted, they should be conducted in a professional manner permitting candidates adequate opportunity for explaining and demonstrating their qualifications.

8. Departments inviting candidates for on-campus interviews should pay candidates' expenses, in accord with standard institutional policies for travel reimbursement. Candidates should be told approximately how many candidates are being invited for on-campus interviews.

9. No candidate may be required before 15 January to make a final answer to an offer of a position without tenure for the following academic year. From 15 January to the middle of summer, candidates should normally be allowed two weeks for a final answer to a formal offer.

Statement on Applications

The following statement on acknowledging applications from job seekers is based on a motion passed by the Delegate Assembly in December 1982 and approved by the Executive Council in May 1983:

Acting on a recommendation from the MLA Delegate Assembly, the MLA Executive Council has adopted a policy calling for departments to acknowledge all applications for announced positions either by letter or by self-addressed postcards provided by applicants.

Statement on the Use of Part-Time Faculty

The following statement on the use of part-time faculty was developed by an ad hoc committee of the Association of Departments of English and adopted by the MLA Executive Council in May 1982:

The recent dramatic increase in the use of part-time teachers in many departments of English and foreign languages is already threatening departmental integrity, professional standards, and academic excellence. Although some part-time appointments add significant dimensions to curricula and some professionals prefer to accept only part-time academic appointments because of other commitments, most part-time appointments are not made for educationally sound reasons. Indeed, the primary motivation for many of these appointments has been to reduce the cost of instruction.

From the point of view of the departmental administrator, part-time teachers fall into two general groups. Most are clearly temporary members of a department. Others teach from year to year and become virtually permanent. Graduate students who serve as apprentice teachers enjoy a special status in their departments and are therefore distinct from these groups.

The very conditions under which most temporary and permanent part-time teachers are employed define them as nonprofessionals. Often they are hired quickly, as last-minute replacements, with only hasty review of their credentials. They receive little recognition or respect for their contributions to their departments; in many instances they are paid inequitably.

The potential damage to academic programs caused by the excessive use of part-time teachers cannot be calculated exactly, but some negative effects are unavoidable. Because part-time teachers are not treated as members of the departmental community, they often have a limited commitment to the institution and its students. Because part-time teachers rarely participate, as professionals should, in the development of courses, the continuity of sequential courses and the consistency of multisectioned courses suffer. Because part-time teachers are rarely available to advise students or, if available, may not be fully informed about institutional programs, inordinately heavy responsibility for advising falls to the full-time faculty. In addition, because of the low professional standing of part-time teachers, their frequent assignment to composition and introductory language courses diminishes the importance of basic courses at a time when society recognizes a need for special attention to this part of the curriculum.

In the face of present conditions and concern about the decline in quality of humanities programs, the MLA urges college and university administrations to make new and concerted efforts to eliminate the excessive use of part-time teachers, to improve the conditions under which part-time teachers are employed, and to recognize the professional status and important contributions of such teachers. Continuation of excessive, unplanned use of part-time teachers can only exacerbate administrative difficulties, invite student dissatisfaction, and threaten the quality of education. The MLA offers the following guidelines for the employment of part-time teachers.

Guidelines

1. *Each department should develop a long-range plan that clarifies the use of both temporary and permanent part-time teachers in terms of departmental needs and goals.* This plan should establish an appropriate limit on how many part-time teachers may be hired in relation to the number of full-time faculty and graduate students who serve as apprentice teachers.

2. *All part-time teachers should be treated as professionals.* They should be hired and reviewed according to processes broadly comparable to those established for full-time faculty. They should be given mailboxes, office space, and clerical support. They should receive adequate introduction to their teaching assignments, departments, and institutions. They should either be paid a pro rata salary or receive a just salary that accurately reflects their teaching duties and an additional stipend for any duties outside the classroom they are asked to assume. When appropriate and in accordance with well-thought-out policies, part-time teachers should participate in determining departmental policies and in planning the courses they teach.

3. *If there is a recurrent need for the services of part-time teachers, departments should consider establishing a cadre of permanent part-time teachers.* In addition to the privileges outlined in item 2, above, these teachers should receive appropriate fringe benefits and incentives that foster professional development, for example, merit raises and access to research and travel funds.

Resolution on Convention Interviews

In December 1984 the Delegate Assembly proposed a resolution, which was approved by the MLA membership on a special ballot in the spring of 1985, urging all departments intending to invite candidates for interviews at the MLA convention to do so as soon as possible and in any case no later than ten days before the beginning of the convention.

Recommendation on Rankings of Students

In April 1985, the MLA Committee on Careers made the following recommendation:

> The Committee on Careers thinks that it is inconsistent with the standards of fairness and impartiality supported by the MLA for a department chair or director of graduate studies to provide rankings of graduate students to potential employers beyond those recommendations contained in dossiers. The hiring departments must make their own rankings on the basis of dossiers provided by candidates.

New policy statements are regularly considered by the ADE, ADFL, and MLA; news of statements under consideration or recently adopted is published in the *MLA Newsletter*, the *Bulletins* of the ADE and ADFL, *Profession*, *PMLA*, and the *Job Information Lists*. These proposed new policies—and other questions and problems related to hiring— normally provide the focus for several sessions and workshops at the MLA annual convention and at the summer seminars of the ADE and ADFL. Newly appointed chairs and chairs undertaking faculty recruitment for the first time will probably find these professional meetings an invaluable source of practical information, expert advice, and peer-group support.

ADVICE ON RECRUITING AND HIRING

As the guidelines suggest, the first step for a department trying to recruit a new faculty member should be to describe the opening in the *Job Information List* for the appropriate field, English or foreign languages. The MLA publishes the *Lists* four times a year, in October, December, February, and April. At an appropriate time about six weeks beforehand, the MLA sends a letter requesting information to all English, foreign language, and related departments. The mailing includes a form for the responses, sample entries, information about deadlines in the current year, and a return envelope. There is no charge to departments for their advertisements.

Appropriate notices are also accepted from nonacademic employers. Any potential employer of PhDs or ABDs in English or foreign languages who does not receive regular requests from the MLA should write or telephone MLA headquarters. Last-minute entries can be telephoned and will be printed if possible.

How to Use the *Job Information Lists*

In writing your statements, be precise and specific.

1. If you have a definite vacancy, say so without ambiguity, and describe the position in detail so that candidates will know whether their qualifications fit your needs. State the rank, or at least indicate whether it is a lower-level or upper-level position; list the degree, the area(s) of specialization, and any other credentials you require. If you will not consider ABDs or candidates without teaching experience or publications, make these criteria clear; it will save you time, and candidates will appreciate your candor. Give a deadline for receipt of applications, and, if you wish, ask candidates to include a self-addressed card for acknowledgment.

2. If you are reasonably sure you will have a vacancy, say so, but add that it is still not a certainty; either invite letters or ask candidates to wait until you have more definite information. Again, give as much detail as you can about the position, the requirements, and the qualifications sought.

3. If you do not know whether you will be able to hire, say so, and tell candidates you will provide more information in the next issue of the *List*.

4. If you know for sure that you will be unable to make an appointment of any kind, say so; lists of departments reporting no vacancies are published in the October and February *Lists*.

5. If you have any other messages to communicate to job seekers—about the status of previously announced jobs, plans for the future, or the likelihood of last-minute part-time openings, for example—use the *List* to publish them.

Your response to letters of inquiry and to applications should correspond to your statement in the *Job Information List*. Try especially to avoid procedures that look unfair. Candidates who respond promptly to a job notice should not be told that applications are no longer being accepted or that the position has already been filled. Candidates who meet the requirements stated in the notice should not be told that they have the wrong qualifications. If the advertisement states that a medievalist is needed and you hire a different specialist without reopening the search, or if it states that a PhD in hand is required and you hire an ABD, scores of candidates will rightly feel that they have been treated unfairly.

If you have advertised no vacancy and a position suddenly opens just after the deadline for a notice in the *List*, you may wish to delay the recruitment process until the next *List*. Obviously, it is in the department's interest to fill vacancies by selecting from all available candidates. When local circumstances make delay impossible in the late fall, you can post last-minute announcements at the MLA convention and reach those candidates who already have appointments for interviews or who are using the Job Information Center for other reasons. You can also advertise in the Sunday *New York Times* and the *Chronicle of Higher Education*, both of which appear weekly; they are expensive and do not serve language and literature candidates as effectively as the *Lists*, but it is worth making an effort to reach candidates. Every time an unannounced vacancy is filled, the cynicism about the ethics of our profession grows more bitter.

To reassure candidates that the information in the *List* is up-to-date and accurate, write a new statement with the current date for each issue of the *List*, even if there has been no change in your situation.

Finally, be sure you allow candidates sufficient time to apply for a position you have described in the *List*—at least twenty-one days after the announcement appears. If you wish to set a deadline for receipt of applications, be sure it is reasonable and include it in the announcement.

Screening Applicants and Scheduling Interviews

The procedures used by departments in hiring new faculty vary according to the size of the department and the budget available for recruitment, as well as to the traditions of the institution and the personal preferences of the chair. Unexpected resignations or late authorizations to hire can disrupt orderly planning. The suggestions that follow must be adapted to particular circumstances, but they apply to the most common cases.

If your statement in the *List* has clearly described the position to be filled, a quick screening of letters of application should separate the qualified from the unqualified candidates. For screening letters, it is usually preferable to have a small committee; such a committee should work rapidly when many letters are coming in, to decide which candidates should submit dossiers. A large department with several vacancies might use a different committee for each job. Since the principal task at this stage is to read the letters and vitas, the committee may not need to meet but can return written votes to the chair.

As the screening process continues, applicants should be told as promptly as possible how they stand. It is cowardice, not kindness, to postpone informing candidates who have been dropped from consideration. Every applicant should receive a signed personal letter, although it is probably better not to offer explanations to candidates eliminated at an early stage. Whatever reason is offered may seem like an invitation to write an appeal. A brief courteous letter such as the example in appendix C would suffice. Applicants still in the running should receive an explanation of the stages remaining in the screening process.

In requesting dossiers, make it clear that you are still screening applicants and that the request does not guarantee an interview. Acknowledge dossiers as soon as they arrive, and inform candidates as soon as possible whether you wish to interview them (see the sample letters in appendix C). Since candidates may go to some expense to attend interviews, do not schedule an interview unless there is a realistic possibility that the job will materialize and unless the candidate has a realistic chance of getting it.

In arranging interviews, be sure to give candidates adequate notice of the time and exact location of the interview. This information is particularly important if you are interviewing at the MLA annual convention, where it is extremely difficult for candidates to locate chairs through hotel switchboards. Making final arrangements by phone before the convention enables you to iron out small difficulties and ensures against misunderstandings. It gives you and the candidate an opportunity to exchange useful information and mutual assurance.

At the convention, you may find it convenient to conduct interviews in the Job Information Center interview area; if instead you prefer to interview in your hotel room, be sure to register your room number at the sign-in desk in the Job Information Center, so that it can be given to candidates with whom you have scheduled interviews. If you wish, you can give the person on duty a list of the candidates to be interviewed, so that your room number is not passed out indiscriminately.

Many colleges and universities require departments to keep records of their recruitment experiences in order to document the fairness of the procedures, especially with respect to affirmative action and equal opportunity guidelines. The local administration will supply guidance about the information to be gathered and reported. Even if no records are required, it is wise to maintain a list of all applications received and to keep track of the correspondence with each applicant. If, as is desirable, several people read the applications and dossiers, a standard evaluation form helps focus attention on the important criteria; these forms should also be kept and will provide evidence that the search was equitably conducted, should its fairness be challenged later.

Interviews

Interviews can be either harrowing or enjoyable experiences for job candidates—and for interviewers. Much of what occurs depends on the chair who conducts the interview or presides over the search committee. If you are pleasant, relaxed, and forthright, you can do a great deal to put candidates at their ease and to help them project their best image.

Before scheduling interviews, you should decide what you hope to learn from the encounter, especially if the interview is to be done by a team. It is generally pointless to have the candidate repeat the information in the dossier. Ideally, you would discover something of the person's self-presentation as a colleague and as a teacher, and you would be able to assess how his or her qualities would suit the particular needs of your department and institution. By the time of the interview, you should have in mind a specific list of areas of inquiry or qualities you are looking for, and perhaps some specific questions to probe for each one.

In scheduling the interviews, take care not to overload your own schedule. You will learn more if you begin each one reasonably fresh and with the individual candidate's dossier clear in your mind. You should allow enough time between interviews to write down your evaluation and comments.

Encourage the candidates to talk, but don't let them run away with the interview to the extent that you lose the opportunity to ask important questions. Be sure that your own list of priorities has been covered.

Be clear and concise about your requirements and expectations. If your department emphasizes research and publication in addition to good teaching, let the candidate know, and direct some of your questions to the candidate's progress on the dissertation, on revising the dissertation for publication, or on directions for future research. If you are looking for distinctive skills (such as the ability to work with a particular type of student, to teach extension or interdisciplinary courses, or to direct multisection courses), make this requirement clear, and ask the candidate to relate some experiences in the area. By and large, factual information can be communicated more efficiently in writing; in the face-to-face contact, you should try to form an opinion about the candidate as a person—and remember that the candidate is forming a similar opinion about you.

Don't commit yourself to making an offer unless specifically authorized to do so. Tell candidates that you cannot make an offer or promise an offer without approval from the appropriate departmental committee or the dean. If there will be additional stages in the screening process, such as a campus visit, mention them. Be as open as possible about what you are doing; explain how many candidates are still under consideration, when the decisions will be made, and what the most important factors seem to be. If you can, give an opinion about the candidate's chances, but state clearly that you are not binding yourself.

Don't demand acceptance of an offer within an unreasonably short time, certainly not during the interview. The candidate should receive the offer in writing, with all the details spelled out, and should have time to think it over before deciding. Even if you bully the candidate into a premature acceptance, it will be difficult to enforce the agreement if he or she gets a better offer—and if you have pushed too hard, other offers may look better than they are.

At the end of the interview, give the candidates at least an approximate date when they can expect to hear something from you. At the same time, ask them to inform you if, in the interim, they receive another offer, especially if they intend to accept it.

Several years ago, the Job Information Service of the MLA drew up a list of dos and don'ts for interviewers. Although some of them repeat the advice just given, the document is worth quoting in full:

Dos and Don'ts for Interviewers

The job interview is an event that has caused sufficient anxiety for both interviewer and interviewee to prompt a number of publications dealing with the topic. In recent years, concern about discrimination in the hiring process has led to a heightened awareness of the possibility of discriminatory intent in the questions asked by interviewers. In order to facilitate the conduct of interviews arranged through the MLA Job Information Service, guidelines have been developed for both interviewers and job candidates. The "Dos and Don'ts" for interviewers are reproduced below.

Do	Don't
Read résumé in advance	Ask about age
Review job requirements	Ask about marital status
Outline points to be covered	Ask about children
Ensure freedom from interruption	Ask about religion
Establish and maintain a pleasant atmosphere	Ask about national origin
	Display boredom
Explain operation of school and department	Doodle
	Produce stress intentionally

Do	Don't
Describe working conditions – course load, other duties, salary, etc.	Argue with candidate
	Be or appear hostile to candidate
Elicit reasons for candidate's interest in this particular job	Be patronizing
	Ask for information already in dossier
Be polite and courteous	Ask leading questions
Try to put candidate at ease	Ask yes or no questions, if they can be avoided
Be aware of your own biases	
Ask specific questions to elicit facts	Get off on tangents
Elicit all relevant information	Do all the talking
Explore areas such as education, experience, special interests or skills, future expectations	Describe the job in negative terms
	Oversell the position
	Downgrade other institutions
Discuss candidate's attitude toward composition or language teaching and literary research	Intimidate candidate or prevent candidate from asking questions
	Make job offer until all interviews are concluded
Try to ascertain language abilities	
Assess candidate's strengths and weaknesses	
Maintain eye contact	
Allow candidate's questions	
Make sure to listen carefully	
Ask follow-up questions for clarification or further details	
Provide candidate with clear picture of job	

Final Selection

After you and/or your colleagues have met with all the candidates with whom you scheduled interviews, call a meeting of the appropriate faculty group to discuss the qualifications of each candidate. As a result of this discussion, draw up a ranked list of the most promising candidates for the position. If time and funds permit and if the job warrants the effort, you may want to invite the top two or three candidates to your campus for interviews, supplying them beforehand with a detailed schedule for the visit. Let them know, for example, if they will be expected to give a lecture to the department, to make a presentation to a class, or to meet with the faculty selection committee, the dean, or other administrators. Your institution should be prepared to pay all the major travel expenses for the visit. Such visits demand a good deal of planning and coordination; a candidate who has traveled some distance is entitled to a cordial welcome in addition to the business part of the visit. The candidate will be looking your department and campus over at the same time you are deciding whether to offer the job; you should try to give a good impression. Bear in mind also that campus visits inevitably raise high hopes in the candidates; those who are unsuccessful should be treated with extra tact.

When you make a decision, inform your first choice immediately. Unless the candidate cannot be reached, telephone the offer first and follow it up at once with a formal letter. In the letter of appointment, make sure that you include everything the candidate should know; omissions, intentional or inadvertent, can lead to bitterness and even to lawsuits. State unambiguously the salary, the length of the appointment, the rank, the policy on renewal and promotion, courses to be taught, teaching load, and so forth, and enclose all departmental and institutional documents (including those describing benefits) that might be helpful. Urge candidates to reply as soon as possible, but allow them at least two weeks to consider your offer.

After you have received an acceptance, notify the unsuccessful candidates on your final list immediately. At this stage, anything less than a warm personal letter is inexcusable.

Conclusion

The hiring process ends when the offer has been made and accepted. The department chair would be well advised, however, to plan carefully for the orientation of new faculty. The first year may be a difficult period of transition for new PhDs, and ABDs may find it hard to adjust to a full-time job with their theses still to be written. An effort to welcome newcomers hospitably and to provide them with some friendly counsel about local concerns and customs will avoid many problems.

It is equally important to supervise, evaluate, and advise junior members of the faculty throughout their periods of probation. Regular conferences between the chair and each nontenured faculty member should be scheduled, and the chair should tell junior people how they are doing. Finally, if it becomes necessary to deny reappointment or tenure, the department should offer whatever help it can in the job search.

- Use the *MLA Job Information Lists*.
- Observe the guidelines and policy statements adopted by the MLA, ADE, and ADFL.
- Inform candidates of hiring plans through the *Lists*.
- Avoid hiring candidates who do not present the qualifications advertised.
- Avoid hiring for unadvertised positions.
- Use a committee to screen applicants.
- Notify candidates promptly about their status.
- Arrange interviews early.
- Keep records of the search.
- Plan for interviews.
- Inform candidates about the job.
- Do not pressure candidates.
- When the procedures have been completed, make the decisions as fast as possible.
- Allow candidates reasonable time to respond.
- When the job has been filled, notify other candidates immediately.

ADVICE ON PLACING CANDIDATES

Preparing graduate students for the job market begins the moment they enter graduate school. A department offering a PhD program must of course provide courses covering the fundamentals of the discipline, but it must also offer professional training. Traditionally, graduate departments have mounted a placement campaign for students finishing their work in residence; this section will offer some suggestions for improving that effort.

First, however, we want to indicate how graduate departments can give their graduate students a professional orientation from the start.

Virtually all academic jobs require teaching. A graduate department should furnish teaching opportunities for graduate students, but it is certainly not sufficient simply to send the inexperienced teacher into a classroom full of undergraduates. The opportunity to teach should include orientation and training beforehand, as well as supervision and evaluation during the teaching. At least one member of the graduate faculty ought to have expertise in teaching—that is, knowledge of research and current theories, familiarity with new technology and textbooks, membership in the professional associations that emphasize pedagogy. This person should work in close coordination with the directors of multisectioned courses in which graduate students serve as teaching assistants. The broader the range of experience available, the more valuable it will be. Departments should explore the possibility of having graduate students teach in nearby institutions, including high schools and two-year colleges.

A graduate faculty almost always possesses a vast amount of professional knowledge that remains largely invisible. Faculty members discuss their research in class and demonstrate their teaching by example but rarely invite graduate students into their confidence on their other activities. Some professors pass on this knowledge privately to their advisees, but it can also be imparted more efficiently for all in workshops or seminars. Some possible topics might be fellowships and grants, journal editing, conferences and conventions, professional organizations, and publishing. Ask members of the faculty who have recently held a fellowship or who edit a journal or who are active in a professional association to describe their activities and to answer questions.

Many graduate departments have graduate student organizations of some kind. These clubs often do little more than sponsor social events and serve as grievance committees. They can render much greater service to everyone if they provide opportunities for students to exercise a certain amount of professional initiative. Encourage the organization to invite speakers; make sure the faculty supports the event by attending but does not usurp all the speaker's time and attention. Encourage students also to give public presentations of their own work; some graduate student organizations have published journals of their own. Provide financial assistance from the department budget for worthwhile projects.

The department should of course have its own program of outside speakers. Include some nonacademic speakers, if possible; a PhD from your department who has succeeded in business or government work may have extremely useful information to give and simply by appearing will convey a significant message. These public lectures should be followed, whenever possible, by a reception of some kind, where both faculty and students will have a chance to talk to the guest. If funds permit, consider inviting someone for a more extended visit, to join a class for one meeting or to meet students in small groups during a day or two.

Every advanced graduate student will no doubt have a thesis director, who is by default the student's mentor. The chair, or perhaps the director of graduate students, should oversee these relations to some extent. Give the faculty some guidance about mentoring, and prod them to take their responsibility seriously. If a particular faculty member is hopelessly out of touch with the profession, be sure that students can turn to someone else for advice on practical questions. Ideally, the mentor would analyze the student's credentials as early as possible and suggest ways to improve them. In later stages, the mentor would actively assist the candidate in the job search, not only writing a strong letter but also helping to compile an impressive dossier, making sure the deadlines are met, using personal networks whenever possible, advising the candidate at each step, and so forth. Not every faculty member will be able to provide good mentoring; some of those who could will be overworked or away on leave. The department chair and other administrators should ensure that the mentoring is available through the placement committee, the graduate director, or the chair, for any student who needs it.

A graduate student or recent PhD looking for a job will have a much stronger vita if it includes some publications. Advice on the procedures and encouragement from professors to submit a promising paper are indispensable, but some financial assistance would also be helpful. Faculty members usually have access either to departmental typing services or to research grants from the university; similar funds would make it easier for graduate students to revise and to make photocopies. For those whose dissertations might be published as monographs, a more generous publication subsidy might be considered. Especially in foreign languages, university presses have sharply cut back their publishing programs; the monograph series that have taken up the responsibility usually require the author to pay a substantial part of the cost, amounting to several thousand dollars. Some institutions will defray these costs for junior faculty. For unemployed or part-time faculty, the expense is very large, yet it may well mean the difference between survival and failure in the academic world. Graduate schools might reasonably consider aid in such cases as part of the general preparation for success in the profession.

Travel support would be even more widely useful to graduate students, especially at the point when they must go to conventions for interviews. Again, at least limited travel funds are usually available for faculty to travel to give papers or perform official functions at scholarly meetings. Students should be encouraged in the same activities, and funds should be made available to help them meet their expenses.

Specific Placement Services

In addition to general programs that help prepare students for their careers, graduate departments can provide several specific services during the final stages of the search.

1. The department chair and other faculty should familiarize themselves with this *Guide* and with the *Job Information Lists*. Make sure that all job candidates in the department have easy access to copies of both the *Guide* and current issues of the *Lists*. The two thousand or so departments belonging to the Association of Departments of English (ADE) and Association of Departments of Foreign Languages (ADFL) receive copies of each issue of the relevant list as a benefit of membership, but other departments may subscribe separately. Urge job candidates who wish to subscribe individually to the *Lists* to do so by the middle of September, so as to receive the October issue as soon as it is published.

2. Provide candidates with sample letters of application containing the essential information prospective employers should have. Advise candidates that the letter should be not merely a cover letter for the accompanying vita sheet but a personalized statement of the candidate's teaching experience, special qualifications, interests, and goals (see samples in appendix C). You may wish to supply anonymous and suitably edited examples of a range of well-prepared (and poorly prepared) letters from the department's files.

3. Draw up a model curriculum vitae (see samples in appendix C), remembering that not all candidates know what format to use and what information to include. Be sure to advise candidates to supply all essential information; for example, it is annoying for

prospective employers not to know dissertation titles or directors' names. Information about courses taught, honors, publications if appropriate, travel abroad (especially for foreign language candidates), and special training and skills should all be included—in short, the full range of academic experience as it reflects the candidate's interests and competencies.

4. Make sure that you, as well as your candidates, know what your placement bureau requires for a complete dossier, and at your first departmental meeting each fall devote some time to discussing with your colleagues the problems involved in writing effective letters of recommendation. Warn against vague generalities and undue stress on minor weaknesses. It may be useful to hand out some anonymous and suitably edited letters from the department's files, illustrating both valuable and useless recommendations.

5. Opinions differ about whether chairs should attempt to review the letters of recommendation in their candidates' dossiers. While it would be improper for the chair to dictate an opinion or censor the letters, there is obvious value in having a second person read them before they go out to other chairs, simply to scan for unintentional negativity or unfortunate phrasing. Many members of the profession, moreover, regard it as unethical for a faculty member to put a critical letter into a student's file when the student has no way to know of its existence; yet some professors do so. The chair is usually the only person who might watch for such letters and ask to have them withdrawn.

Departments will have to decide their own policy on this question. Whatever decision is reached, chairs or placement directors should make certain that their colleagues know what constitutes an effective letter and should offer encouragement and assistance in writing recommendations. If the majority support it, some system of monitoring should be established. Some writers still seem unaware of current conditions in the job market, and because everyone occasionally slips into irrelevance, vagueness, rhetorical inflation, or even unfairness, it may be wise to seek regular means of avoiding these flaws in the crucially important letters of recommendation.

6. Working with the graduate student association, call early in each semester a meeting of all probable job seekers and all faculty members involved in placement and hiring (placement director, director of graduate studies, director of teaching assistants, personnel or search committee members). Invite all graduate students to attend. While one purpose of these meetings will be to provide information to job seekers, make sure that there is an open exchange among all students and faculty in attendance. Graduate students in their second year of job hunting can often contribute a great deal to these sessions. The winter meeting would be a good situation in which to distribute sample vitas and dossiers and to discuss advance planning; the September meeting would focus on the *Job Information Lists*, letters of application, the forthcoming convention, and interviews.

In these or other meetings, be sure that candidates are aware of conditions and responsibilities in institutions other than PhD-granting universities. Members of the junior staff or chairs from neighboring institutions—including state colleges, liberal arts colleges, comprehensive colleges, and two-year colleges—can make important contributions toward preparing new candidates for the job search. It is unrealistic and unfair to groom graduate students only for positions in other graduate departments; they should be prepared for the kinds of jobs they are most likely to be offered.

7. After the meetings, set aside time to meet with the candidates individually to discuss problems and answer additional questions. Encourage them to have their advisers check their vitas, dossier materials, and letters of application. Further general meetings of can-

didates with the chair or smaller groups of faculty may be profitable if candidates submit drafts of their vitas and letters for suggestions and discussion.

8. Mock interviews for candidates entering the job market for the first time are almost indispensable. Students can take turns playing the interviewer, and second-year job seekers can furnish examples of real questions and situations. Telephone conversations as well as face-to-face interviews should be rehearsed. Experience is by far the best teacher for interviewees, but it is painful to learn the hard way when jobs are scarce.

9. Encourage the whole faculty to take responsibility for placing all the current job seekers. When a candidate seems to have a good chance at a given job, the faculty can often help by providing information about the institution or by writing directly to friends on the faculty there. Colleagues should therefore keep one another informed about the current status of the job search of their advisees and should volunteer useful suggestions whenever possible. A generally good record in placing candidates is one of the strongest attractions of a graduate program, and a network of former students on other faculties is a major means of recruiting students and a fundamental source of a department's power and prestige in the discipline. It is to everyone's advantage to join in efforts to place candidates.

Counseling Job Seekers

1. Be as fully informed about the job market as possible. Read this *Guide* attentively, and read other materials on job hunting and the current state of the market. Check job listings yourself in the *Job Information Lists*, the *Chronicle of Higher Education*, and other sources, and call them to the attention of suitable candidates. Maintain contacts with former students and other chairs, who will let you know of unexpected openings.

2. Begin the counseling process early. Encourage students to attend meetings about job hunting from their first year on. Be sure that those who should soon be leaving your campus get their vitas, dossiers, and recommenders in order the spring before they have to look actively for positions. Keep a calendar of deadlines, and remind students as the deadlines approach.

3. Make your advice as specific as possible. Review the materials the candidates prepare for themselves, and make specific suggestions for improving them. Be realistic about the candidate's chances and about the job market; encourage students to develop their strengths and to apply for appropriate jobs.

4. Be as supportive as possible. Morale is a serious problem among job seekers in a poor job market. As an administrator, you can often relieve some of the anxieties of waiting by explaining how the procedures function (or fail to function). Give encouragement about any positive signs, such as requests for dossiers or interviews, and minimize the significance of the inevitable disappointments.

5. Be open-minded and encourage open-mindedness in the candidates. Give them a realistic sense of what to expect in other types of institution, but do not impose a hierarchy of prestige or suitability. Make sure that all candidates consider what sort of job their abilities and interests best suit them for and that they include nonacademic jobs in the list.

6. Use your own contacts in the profession, your own personal experience on both sides of the hiring process, your knowledge of the job market. Do everything you can to have your colleagues do the same. The candidates ought to feel that the entire faculty is working to help them find jobs and that no avenue has been neglected.

7. Urge candidates to use the *Job Information Lists* and to abide by the guidelines printed

in the *Lists*, writing only to departments that advertise appropriate job openings or possible openings. Caution against writing letters before the October *List* appears or writing about jobs for which students do not have compatible credentials. Emphasize that the job-seeking and recruitment processes are a cooperative effort between candidates and chairs, both of whom must work within the system in the interest of fairness and efficiency.

8. Advise candidates to indicate in letters of application their availability for interviews at regional and national meetings. Explain the advantages of attending such meetings and participating in them; if possible, candidates should plan to give a paper at the MLA convention, where the largest number of interviews are conducted. Warn candidates, however, that they should not expect to arrange interviews at the convention or through random contacts.

9. Remind candidates to submit individually written and typed letters of application. Emphasize the importance of presentation in both the letters and the vita; professional-quality typing is essential. Encourage them to find out something about the institutions to which they apply and to adapt their letters accordingly. The further they get in the process, the more seriously they should investigate.

10. Point out that the chances of finding a job are greatly improved if the candidate will consider all regions and different types of institution. Remind candidates that most recent PhDs spend several years in temporary jobs before finding a tenure-track position, if they find such a position at all.

11. Discourage graduate students from becoming job candidates if they are not certain that their dissertations will be completed before the time of employment. With the increasing number of experienced PhDs on the market, ABD's are less and less competitive. Moreover, completing the thesis is likely to be far more difficult for a full-time employee deprived of the adviser and the university library. Some job notices specify ABDs, and many graduate students find it difficult to survive without an instructor's income; if conditions permit, however, most candidates ought to wait until the thesis is virtually completed before looking for a job.

12. Go over all the dos and don'ts of interviewing, even the most obvious ("be punctual, well-dressed and well-groomed, courteous, alert, and interested"). Emphasize the importance of candidates' briefing themselves about the department and institution before an interview. Warn them that they may be asked inappropriate, irrelevant, unfair, or hostile questions about religion, marital status, political views, and life-style and that they should decide in advance how to respond to such situations—whether to answer directly, to challenge the question, or to evade it. Urge all candidates to practice in mock interviews before going to a real one.

13. Go over the timing of the hiring process, and remind candidates that they should not expect to receive offers before early spring. They should realize that many departments make offers in May or June and that many others hire right at the start of the term, in August or September. Under no circumstances should they think that the MLA convention in December is the only place to obtain positions.

14. Assure candidates that most chairs are deeply concerned about the employment situation and that those who anticipate openings often experience their own frustrations in trying to learn from the administration if and when they will be permitted to hire. Prepare them for the possibility that the interviewer may be inexperienced or overburdened, and urge them not to be discouraged by a bad experience.

At the MLA Convention

If the department can afford it, provide some financial assistance to candidates who plan to attend the convention. Look into other ways to reduce their travel expenses; perhaps a car pool can be arranged or even a bus chartered if several departments get together.

Ideally, graduate students will have familiarized themselves ahead of time with the MLA and other conventions. If possible, job seekers should try to give a paper. For any candidates who have not previously attended a convention, however, be sure that someone briefs them thoroughly ahead of time. Delegate a fellow student or faculty member to serve as guide at the beginning. The first experience of a large, confusing convention can be intimidating.

Most job seekers will probably stay in the less expensive hotels or with friends rather than in the principal convention hotels. If the department can provide a base of operations for the candidates, it will prove a great help to them and a morale booster. For example, the department might provide a large room or suite in which candidates could rest between interviews, receive messages, and share stories with one another. The placement director might take responsibility for being available there during most of the convention, to take messages, provide advice, help with problems, keep extra copies of documents, perhaps even to run errands or perform other services. Other faculty members who are attending should be encouraged to stop by and give encouragement or help with problems.

All faculty members should be urged to attend and to help the department's graduate students, especially those who are looking for jobs. Experienced members of the profession can render enormous service to newer ones simply by escorting them and by introducing them to colleagues from other institutions. A few words of support can give a big boost to the morale of a weary job seeker. A few minutes spent having coffee or a drink together can give candidates a chance to debrief, to get some advice, and to feel the solidarity of a group.

Appendix A

CURRENT INFORMATION ON EMPLOYMENT OF DOCTORATES IN LANGUAGES AND LITERATURES

Since 1977, at first annually and now biennially, the MLA has compiled job-placement records of all persons who receive PhDs in the discipline during the previous academic year. The survey asks representatives of the PhD-granting departments to provide data on their most recent graduating class of PhDs. The results of each year's survey are published in the ADE and ADFL *Bulletins* and in summary form in the *MLA Newsletter*. The survey of 1983-84, completed in 1985, shows that the number of doctorates awarded has continued to fall since 1977 and that the rates of placement in full-time postsecondary teaching (including temporary positions) and in tenure-track positions have held steady or declined slightly. Generally over the last eight to nine years, the tenure-track placement rate for both English and foreign languages has been above forty percent, the full-time postsecondary teaching rate for both fields has been around sixty percent (with wide variations among the various foreign languages), and the total placement rate, including positions in fields other than college-level teaching, has been over ninety percent.

Results of the 1983-84 survey are displayed in the accompanying table. Figures from English departments appear in the column farthest to the right of the page; figures representing the sum of responses from all fields of foreign language and literature are in the next-to-last column on the right; those from the individual language fields across the page from left to right. Totals showing tenure-track appointments appear on line 4, full-time postsecondary teaching positions on line 7, and total employment rates at the bottom of the page.

MLA SURVEY OF PHD PLACEMENT, 1983–84

	Classics	Comparative Literature	French	German	Other Germanic	Italian	Linguistics	Slavic	Spanish and Portuguese	Arabic	Hebrew	Other Near Eastern	Chinese	Japanese	Other Asian	Total foreign language	English
1. Programs granting PhDs	22	24	44	33	2	11	19	15	45	4	4	7	8	7	2	247	116
2. Programs awarding no PhDs in 1983–84	8	5	21	26	2	5	7	9	18	1	2	1	3	6	3	115	10
3. PhDs granted	51	99	98	77	2	16	84	35	113	7	4	8	15	12	8	629	672
to men	28	40	30	37	0	5	49	16	56	5	3	7	7	4	4	291	290
% men in total	55	40	30	48	—	31	58	46	50	71	75	88	47	33	50	46	43
to women	23	59	68	40	2	11	35	19	57	2	1	1	8	8	4	338	382
% women in total	45	60	70	52	100	69	42	54	50	29	25	12	53	66	—	54	57
4. Tenure-track appts.	19	43	37	24	0	6	28	19	57	2	3	3	4	7	1	253	246
as % of PhDs granted	37	43	38	31	—	38	33	54	24	29	75	38	27	58	12	40	37
men	10	22	16	17	0	5	21	10	31	2	3	3	1	3	1	145	121
% men in tenure track	53	51	43	71	—	83	75	53	54	100	100	100	25	43	100	57	49
women	9	21	21	7	0	1	7	9	26	0	0	0	3	4	0	108	125
% women in tenure track	47	49	57	29	—	17	25	47	46	0	0	0	75	57	—	43	51
5. Non-tenure-track appts.																	
men	6	9	7	8	0	0	9	1	12	0	0	0	0	0	0	52	51
women	4	10	11	7	1	3	5	0	5	0	0	0	2	2	0	50	68
6. Appointments for 1 year																	
men	4	2	1	2	0	0	1	2	2	0	0	0	3	1	1	19	15
women	2	1	7	3	1	1	1	1	2	0	0	0	0	1	0	20	9
7. % of 1983–84 PhDs in full-time academic position																	
all	69	66	64	57	100	63	52	66	69	29	75	38	60	92	25	63	58
men	71	83	80	73	—	100	63	81	80	40	100	43	57	100	50	74	64
women	65	54	57	43	100	46	37	53	58	—	—	—	63	88	—	53	53
8. Part-time appts.																	
men	3	0	1	1	0	0	2	0	1	1	0	2	2	0	2	15	29
women	0	3	5	7	0	0	3	1	3	0	0	0	0	0	0	22	50

	C1		C2		C3		C4		C5		C6		C7		C8		C9		C10		C11		C12		C13		C14		C15	
9. Postdoctoral study																															
men	1		2		0		0		0		0		5		0		1		1		1		0		0		12		1	
women	0		2		0		1		0		0		7		2		0		1		0		0		0		13		3	
10. Secondary schools																															
men	1		0		0		1		0		0		0		0		4		0		0		0		0		6		10	
women	0		2		4		1		0		0		0		0		6		0		0		0		0		13		19	
11. Higher ed. administration																															
men	0		2		0		1		0		0		0		0		0		0		0		0		0		4		3	
women	1		1		0		2		0		0		0		0		0		0		0		0		0		4		13	
12. Government																															
men	1		0		0		1		0		0		2		1		1		0		0		0		0		6		5	
women	0		0		3		0		0		1		1		1		1		1		0		1		0		10		2	
13. Nonprofit orgs.																															
men	0		1		1		2		0		0		0		1		0		0		0		0		0		5		3	
women	2		1		1		2		0		0		1		0		1		0		0		0		0		9		4	
14. Business																															
men	1		2		2		3		0		0		3		1		1		1		0		0		0		14		18	
women	1		0		4		5		0		1		2		2		4		0		0		0		2		22		33	
15. Unemployed—seeking in a specific area																															
men	0		0		1		0		0		0		0		0		0		0		0		0		0		1		5	
women	3		3		7		2		0		1		2		0		2		0		0		0		0		20		25	
16. Unemployed—seeking anywhere																															
men	1		0		1		0		0		0		3		0		0		0		0		0		0		5		11	
women	1		2		1		0		0		2		3		0		1		0		0		0		0		10		7	
17. Unemployed—seeking nonacademic employment																															
men	0		0		0		0		0		0		0		0		0		0		0		0		0		0		3	
women	0		0		0		0		0		0		0		0		0		0		0		0		0		0		1	
18. Unknown or other																															
men	0		2		0		1		0		0		4		0		0		0		0		0		0		7		15	
women	0		11		4		2		0		1		3		3		2		0		1		2		1		30		23	
19. % of PhDs employed	90.2		81.8		85.7		93.5		100		75.0		82.1		91.4		95.6		100		75.0		86.7		87.5		88.4		86.6	
men	96.4		95.0		93.3		97.3		—		100.0		85.7		100.0		100.0		100		100.0		100.0		100.0		95.5		88.3	
women	82.6		72.9		82.4		90.0		100		63.6		77.1		84.2		91.1		100		0.0		75.0		75.0		82.2		85.3	

ADDITIONAL SOURCES OF INFORMATION ABOUT TEACHING AND ADMINISTRATIVE POSITIONS

In addition to considering the sources on this list, candidates should consult their state employment agencies, some of which list academic positions, and ask university placement officers and colleagues for information about reliable private agencies and other possible sources of employment information. (Readers are invited to send information about other sources of job information that should be included in revisions of this pamphlet.)

Academe

Academe, the newsletter of the American Association of University Professors, carries information about teaching and administrative positions in a section entitled "Academic Vacancies." Published in September, December, March, and June, *Academe: The Bulletin of the AAUP* is available for an annual fee of $30 from the AAUP, 1012 14th St., NW, Washington, DC 20005.

American Association of Teachers of French

Membership in the AATF is a prerequisite for registration with its placement bureau. Dues are $21 for the calendar year. A fee of $12.50 (for twelve months) is charged for supplying monthly vacancy lists to candidates; a dossier-handling service is available for $25, including the vacancy lists. For further information, write to the AATF, 57 E. Armory Ave., Champaign, IL 61820.

American Association of Teachers of German

The AATG's Placement Information Centers (PICs) form a nationwide network of volunteer members who facilitate the exchange of information about employment opportunities for specialists in German. The program is not a placement service: no fees are charged, and AATG membership is not required. The PICs concentrate on high school, junior college, and part-time positions, including nonacademic opportunities; they can also respond to emergency personnel needs at any level. Interested job seekers should obtain registration forms from the AATG office, Suite 201, 523 Bldg., Route 38, Cherry Hill, NJ 08034.

American Association of Teachers of Slavic and East European Languages

Positions in Slavic and East European languages are listed in the AATSEEL *Newsletter*, which is published six times a year. *Newsletter* subscriptions are available for an annual fee of $4.50 from AATSEEL, Modern Language Bldg. 340, Univ. of Arizona, Tucson, AZ 85721.

American Association of Teachers of Spanish and Portuguese

Notices of available positions in Spanish and Portuguese are circulated on the average of once a month to AATSP members registered with the association's placement bureau.

An initial registration fee of $15 covers the first year's services, and $10 is charged for yearly renewal of registration. The bureau maintains dossiers of registrants and distributes them on request. For further information, write to Teresa R. Arrington, Director of the AATSP Placement Bureau, Dept. of Modern Languages, Univ. of Mississippi, University, MS 38677.

The *Chronicle of Higher Education*

Published weekly—except for the last two weeks in August and the last two weeks in December—the *Chronicle* includes in each issue a "Bulletin Board," listing under "Positions Available" administrative and teaching vacancies in all fields. Candidates may advertise their availability under "Positions Wanted" for 85¢ per word. Copy and payment for candidate listings should be sent to "Bulletin Board," *Chronicle of Higher Education*, P. O. Box 19446, Washington, DC 20036. Subscriptions to the *Chronicle* are available for $48 (48 issues); add $1 for billing charges if payment does not accompany the order.

Conference on College Composition and Communication

The CCCC operates a placement service for its members in conjunction with its annual convention. A fee of $10 is charged for CCCC members, $14 for nonmembers. Before the convention, department chairs are invited to list vacancies (or to indicate that they have no vacancies), and members seeking positions are invited to register with the service. Lists of available candidates and of jobs are then distributed on request before the meeting. At the meeting, the CCCC provides a meeting room, a file of convention addresses for registrants and chairs in attendance, and bulletin boards on which notices and notes can be posted. For further information, write to CCCC Placement Service, 1111 Kenyon Road, Urbana, IL 61801.

Commercial Teacher Agencies

Advertisements from commercial teacher agencies, which generally charge a registration fee as well as a substantial placement fee, appear regularly in the *New York Times* and other newspapers. Although located in New York, Chicago, or other urban centers, many agencies work by mail in an attempt to provide national and even international coverage in their listings of positions.

Council for Advancement and Support of Education

The CASE *Placement Letter*, published monthly except September and January, includes information about staffing needs at educational institutions in fund-raising, alumni administration, government relations, institutional relations, periodicals, and publications. Degrees or special training and skills in journalism and communications are desirable for many positions. College administrative experience is also highly desirable. Individuals in, or seeking to enter, the field may advertise their availability in the *Placement Letter* for a minimum charge of $12.50. Subscription rates are $12.50 for five issues or $20 annually, with complimentary copies to advertisers in each issue. For further information, write to Weslie Stubbs, *Placement Letter*, CASE, Suite 400, 11 Dupont Circle, NW, Washington, DC 20036.

Higher Education Administration and Referral Service

HEARS operates a year-round referral service to aid colleges and universities seeking administrative staff in the areas of records, registration, admissions, institutional research, financial aid, and other university support positions. While the service is open to all candidates who wish to place their names on file, it should be noted that most positions listed call for at least some administrative experience. There is a yearly registration fee for job candidates; the fee is waived for members in certain affiliate categories. For further information, write to HEARS, Suite 510, 1 Dupont Circle, NW, Washington, DC 20036.

The *New York Times*

The *New York Times* Sunday edition, section 4, has a page or more of advertisements for teaching and administrative positions in schools, colleges, and universities. Advertisements in the Sunday *Times* are not limited to the New York area.

Teaching Opportunities Abroad

The counseling division of the Institute of International Education advises,

Requirements for teaching abroad, as to educational background, previous teaching experience, language ability, age, and certification, vary depending on the program. The length of appointments also varies; cultural exchange awards are usually tenable for an academic year, while some other programs require a commitment of several years. In general, application should be made from six months to a year in advance of the expected appointment date. In each case, specific information should be requested from the administering agency.

Teaching Abroad, a comprehensive listing of sources of information about teaching opportunities throughout the world, is available for $11.95 from the IIE, 890 United Nations Plaza, New York, NY 10017.

Appendix C
SAMPLE LETTERS AND FORMS

The résumés and letters of application included in appendix C have been constructed with the same fictional person in mind: a job candidate in English who spent two years completing the MA degree and expects to receive the PhD in June 1986. This person taught in a high school for one year after receiving the BA and for two years while working on the master's and served as a teaching assistant while completing the PhD. These sample résumés and letters are intended only to suggest possible formats and styles and to illustrate ways in which a candidate may emphasize different aspects of his or her background in applications to different prospective employers.

In tailoring a résumé to a particular type of institution or employer, candidates should consider making certain adjustments—for example, rearranging topics on the résumé; providing detailed information for some items and only a summary for others; emphasizing breadth of experience, including nonacademic work, instead of concentrating on academic research and teaching. The needs of the large state university are not necessarily those of the prestigious research institution; the skills that would be most appropriate to the hiring department at a selective liberal arts college may not be so important at a community college. Letters of application should also stress those aspects of the candidate's education and experience that most closely suit the stated needs of the prospective institution or employer. It cannot be emphasized too strongly that there is no standard content or wording for either a résumé or a letter of application.

LETTER OF APPLICATION:
FOUR-YEAR COLLEGE OR UNIVERSITY

3920 South University Avenue
Essex, NJ 08875
29 November 1985

Professor Janet R. Walters, Chair
Department of English
Cartesian University
Randolph, IN 47915

Dear Professor Walters:

I am writing in response to your description in the December <u>MLA Job Information List</u> of a possible assistant professorship for a PhD with a strong interest in British literature before 1850.

I am currently completing my dissertation (two chapters have already been accepted by my committee) and expect to have the PhD in hand by June 1986. As noted in the enclosed vita, I am writing on "The Mock Heroic as a Convention before Dryden." The purpose of the study is to show that many of the conventions Dryden used had also been employed by British poets before him, particularly by Chaucer, Beaumont and Fletcher, and Butler; the thesis focuses on the allusive nature of mock-heroic poetry and on the structure of early mock-heroic poems. My scholarly interests also include the Metaphysical poets, and I have had an article on "Holy Sonnet XI" accepted for publication in the <u>Donne Society Quarterly</u>.

In addition to my research, I have been deeply involved in teaching composition, both in the traditional classroom and in a laboratory setting. In Eastern University's Writing Skills Center I developed a system of individualized instruction that is still in use there. My varied teaching responsibilities, in literature as well as in composition, have prepared me to undertake the teaching duties described in your notice.

My dossier is available on request. I would be pleased to meet with you for an interview during the MLA convention in December, or elsewhere at your convenience. Should you wish to get in touch with me before the convention, I can be reached at the above address until 19 December. After that date I will be at 1313 Elmwood Road, Bay City, OH 57932 (tel.: 607 543-6789).

Thank you for your consideration. I look forward to hearing from you in the near future.

Sincerely yours,

Dale R. Edwards

CURRICULUM VITAE:
FOUR-YEAR COLLEGE OR UNIVERSITY

Curriculum Vitae

Dale R. Edwards
3920 South University Avenue
Essex, NJ 08875
(201) 792-0324

EDUCATION:
1983-86: PhD (expected), English, Eastern Univ., Essex, New Jersey
Major field of concentration: 17th-century British poetry
MA, English, Southwestern Univ., Needham, California
BA, cum laude, Middletown Coll., Madison, Ohio
Major: English; minor: French

DISSERTATION (in progress):
"The Mock Heroic as a Convention before Dryden." The dissertation traces the development of mock-heroic and mock-epic conventions in English poetry before the publication of "MacFlecknoe" in 1682. Dissertation director: Harrison E. Smith

ACADEMIC HONORS:
A. Marshall Elliott Dissertation Fellowship, Eastern Univ., 1985-86
PhD Qualifying Examinations passed with Distinction, 1985
Distinguished Teaching Award, Eastern Univ., 1984
Sigma Tau Delta English Honorary Society, Middletown Coll., 1972-73
Dean's List, Middletown Coll., 1976-80

TEACHING EXPERIENCE:
Freshman Composition, Eastern Univ., 4 semesters
Introduction to Modern Fiction, Eastern Univ., 1 semester
British Literature to 1800, Eastern Univ., 1 semester
Writing Skills Center, Eastern Univ., 2 semesters
North City High School, 3 years*

TEACHING INTERESTS:
Renaissance and 17th-century literature, Metaphysical poetry, rhetoric and composition

PUBLICATIONS:
"A Note on Crucifixion Imagery in 'Holy Sonnet XI,'" accepted for publication in the Donne Society Quarterly

ACADEMIC SERVICE:
Member, Freshman English Textbook Selection Committee, Eastern Univ., 1985-86
Officer, English Graduate Student Committee, Eastern Univ., 1984-85

LANGUAGES:
French: excellent speaking, writing, and reading ability
German: reading knowledge

MEMBERSHIPS:
Modern Language Association, Northeast Modern Language Association, Conference on College Composition and Communication

RECOMMENDATIONS:
Professor Harrison E. Smith, English Dept., Eastern Univ.
Professor Elizabeth Lewis, English Dept., Eastern Univ.
Professor Richard Schultz, Chair, English Dept., Southwestern Univ.

CREDENTIALS:
Complete dossier available from Eastern University Placement Office, 1234 Harding Street, Essex, NJ 08875

*optional item; recommended for teaching-oriented institutions

LETTER OF APPLICATION:
COMMUNITY OR JUNIOR COLLEGE

3920 South University Avenue
Essex, NJ 08875
1 March 1986

Professor James Lewis, Head
Division of Humanities
Boonton Community College
Boonton, OH 63452

Dear Professor Lewis:

I am writing to apply for the position you advertised in the February <u>Job Information</u>
<u>List</u>. I believe I have both the required experience as a composition teacher and the
desired knowledge of reading and writing laboratory instruction.

As you will note from the enclosed résumé, my varied teaching experience has prepared
me to deal with a wide range of reading and writing abilities. At the high school
level, I taught freshman English and reading. I was responsible for identifying problem
readers and their reading deficiencies and for managing the reading laboratory. As a
result, I am familiar with reading diagnostic tests and instructional equipment. More
recently, as a teaching assistant at Eastern University, I taught two sections of
standard freshman composition and two designed for students who had failed first-
semester composition. I also worked in the Writing Skills Center at Eastern, where I
adapted remedial reading strategies to my work with problem writers.

My nonacademic activities include three years as undergraduate campus correspondent for
the <u>Bay City Star Register</u>; I wrote articles on campus events and reviews of theatrical
and musical presentations. During my high school teaching career I was appointed
adviser to the school newspaper, and while working on my PhD at Eastern University I
represented graduate students on the freshman English textbook selection committee. I
will take my final PhD oral exam in June and will have the degree in hand before the
opening of school in September 1986.

My dossier is available on request. I would be pleased to meet with you at the CCCC
convention in April or elsewhere at your convenience.

Thank you for your consideration. I look forward to hearing from you soon.

Sincerely yours,

Dale R. Edwards

CURRICULUM VITAE:
COMMUNITY OR JUNIOR COLLEGE

Curriculum Vitae

Dale R. Edwards
3920 South University Avenue
Essex, NJ 08875
(201) 792-0324

EDUCATION: 1983-86: PhD (expected), English, Eastern Univ., Essex, New Jersey
Dissertation topic: "The Mock Heroic as a Convention before Dryden"
1981-83: MA, English, Southwestern Univ., Needham, California
1976-80: BA, English (minor: French), Middletown Coll., Madison, Ohio

HONORS: A. Marshall Elliott Dissertation Fellowship, Eastern Univ., 1985-86
PhD Qualifying Examinations passed with Distinction, Eastern Univ., 1985
Distinguished Teaching Award, Eastern Univ., 1984
Sigma Tau Delta English Honorary Society, Middletown Coll., 1979-80
Dean's List, Middletown Coll., 1976-80

TEACHING EXPERIENCE: 1983-85: Teaching, Eastern Univ.
Composition (4 semesters)
Writing Laboratory (2 semesters)
Introduction to Modern Fiction (1 semester)
Survey of British Literature (1 semester)

1980-83: North City Senior High School, Appleton, California
English, ninth grade
Reading, ninth grade
Drama, ninth and tenth grades

PROFESSIONAL SERVICE: Member, Freshman English Textbook Selection Committee, Eastern Univ., 1985-86
Officer, English Graduate Student Committee, Eastern Univ., 1984-85
Adviser, North City High School Gazette, 1980-81

OTHER WORK EXPERIENCE: 1979-80: Part-time assistant, Madison (Ohio) Public Library
1976-80: Part-time book reviewer and campus reporter for Bay City Star Register, Bay City, Ohio
1976-78: Counselor, Green Acres Day Camp, Bay City, Ohio (full-time summer position)

PUBLICATIONS: Articles and book reviews in the Bay City Star Register
Poems in Middletown Literary Magazine
"A Note on Crucifixion Imagery in 'Holy Sonnet XI,'" accepted for publication in the Donne Society Quarterly

MEMBERSHIPS: Modern Language Association, Northeast Modern Language Association, Conference on College Composition and Communication

RECOMMENDATIONS: Professor Harrison E. Smith, English Dept., Eastern Univ.
Professor Elizabeth Lewis, English Dept., Eastern Univ.
Professor Richard Schultz, Chair, English Dept., Southwestern Univ.
Mr. Jack Moore, Editor, Bay City Star Register

CREDENTIALS: Complete dossier available on request from Eastern University Placement Office, 1234 Harding Street, Essex, NJ 08875

LETTER OF APPLICATION: NONTEACHING POSITION

3920 South University Avenue
Essex, NJ 08875
15 May 1986

Mr. Norman Johnson
Vice-President for Internal Affairs
Midwestern Equipment Suppliers, Inc.
St. Louis, MO 63998

Dear Mr. Johnson:

I am writing in response to your recent advertisement in the St. Louis Post-Dispatch for an Assistant Director of Internal Communications.

Although my most recent employment has been in the field of higher education, I have also had considerable experience in writing and editing. I have written for both newspapers and scholarly journals and have been involved in all stages of the production process--from the writing itself through copyediting, layout, design, printing, and distribution. I have had experience in preparing reports on a wide range of subjects and, during five years of graduate work, have developed skills as a research analyst that, I believe, will enable me to supervise and assist in the writing of Midwestern's production and scheduling reports. Your advertisement also states that personnel experience is desirable, and, as my résumé shows, I have indeed had that kind of experience in a variety of contexts. Communication, in all its aspects, is my major interest and concern, and I thus feel I could serve you effectively as Assistant Director of Internal Communications.

I would be happy to meet with you to discuss my background and qualifications for the position in more detail and will telephone you early next week to see if we can arrange an appointment. Thank you for your consideration.

Sincerely yours,

Dale R. Edwards

Encl.

BUSINESS RÉSUMÉ

Dale R. Edwards
3920 South University Avenue
Essex, NJ 08875
(201) 792-0324

<u>Professional Goal</u>: A responsible position in communications where use can be made of my writing and editing skills, my managerial experience and analytical abilities, and my capacity for originating and developing ideas.

<u>Writing and Editing Skills</u>: Six years of experience as a writer and editor. As editor, I have supervised writing instruction for more than two hundred high school and college students, have served as the supervisor for all aspects of preparing and distributing a high school newspaper, and have served on a departmental composition-textbook selection committee. I have also written for scholarly publications (the <u>Donne Society Quarterly</u>) and for popular publications (as a reporter and book reviewer for the <u>Bay City Star Register</u>).

<u>Creative Experience</u>: As supervisor of a high school newspaper, I improved the system of bookkeeping and cut printing costs by using different contractors at various stages of production. As a member of the Eastern University Graduate Student Association, I negotiated changes in the graduate curriculum and helped devise a more effective system of student counseling. As a college instructor of writing, I developed a system of individualized instruction that allows each writer to learn at his or her own pace; I also devised a marketing strategy for literature courses by developing a special modern literature program tailored to the expressed interests of students.

<u>Analytical Abilities</u>: Developed through (1) experience during five years in graduate school learning to be a research analyst and (2) work on numerous research projects that required summarizing large amounts of information from diverse sources and recommending the most effective course of action.

<u>Managerial Experience</u>: I have had four years of experience motivating, supervising, and evaluating high school and college students; have served as supervisor of thirty teenagers in summer recreation facilities; have served as credit manager for a large department store, traveling from store to store, making decisions about individual credit applications, and making sure that the credit department performed its duties; have served as an officer in both college and graduate school student organizations.

<u>Special Abilities</u>: I am adept at supervising and motivating personnel and have extensive experience in counseling and advising about performance and future employment plans. I am a trained, analytical reader and have proven skills, documented in my references, as a writer and public speaker.

<u>Work Experience</u>:   1985-86: Research Analyst, Eastern Univ., Essex, New Jersey
1983-85: Instructor in Written Communications and Literature, Eastern Univ., Essex, New Jersey
1980-83: Instructor in Written Communications and Literature and Supervisor of Student Publications, North City Senior High School, Appleton, California
1978-80: Salesperson and then Credit Manager, Brown's Department Stores, Madison, Ohio
1976-78: Reporter for <u>Bay City Star Register</u>, Bay City, Ohio, and (summers) Supervisor of Youth Recreational Facilities, Bay City, Ohio

<u>Education</u>: BA, cum laude, Middletown Coll.; MA, Southwestern Univ.; PhD, Eastern Univ.

References available on request.

NEGATIVE RESPONSE TO APPROPRIATE APPLICATIONS

```
                              CARTESIAN UNIVERSITY
                              Department of English
                              305 Humanities Building


                                         12 December 1985


Mr. Dale R. Edwards
3920 South University Avenue
Essex, NJ 08875

Dear Mr. Edwards:

Our Appointments Committee has now carefully reviewed and evaluated your application,
together with many others we received in response to our notice in the MLA Job
Information List for December. We have narrowed our choice to some ten persons whose
qualifications and background clearly place them at the head of our list, and we must
now regretfully eliminate all other applications, including yours, from consideration.

We appreciate your interest in Cartesian Univesity and wish you well in your search for
a suitable position.

                              Sincerely yours,


                              Janet R. Walters
                              Chair
```

LETTER ARRANGING AN INTERVIEW

                    CARTESIAN UNIVERSITY
                    Department of English
                    305 Humanities Building

                              8 December 1985

Mr. Dale R. Edwards
3920 South University Avenue
Essex, NJ 08875

Dear Mr. Edwards:

After carefully reviewing the dossiers of forty-two candidates, we have narrowed our
selection to the eight individuals whose qualifications are clearly superior. You are
one of those eight candidates, and we would therefore like to interview you at the MLA
convention in New York. Would 3:00 p.m. on Saturday, 28 December, be a convenient time?

At the interview I hope to be joined by two colleagues, Professors Alan McGuire and
Annemarie Schwarz. I plan to stay at the Hyatt Hotel during the convention, but I will
not know my room number in advance. Please check at the main desk in the MLA Job
Information Center when you arrive in Chicago; I will leave word there concerning our
interview location and how you should reach us.

                              Sincerely yours,

                              Janet R. Walters
                              Chair

DATE DUE